AESOP'S
FABLES

COLLINS
CLASSICS

Harper Press
An imprint of HarperCollins*Publishers*
1 London Bridge Street
London SE1 9GF

HarperCollins*Publishers*
1st Floor, Watemarque Building, Ringsend Road,
Dublin 4, Ireland

This Harper Press paperback edition published 2011

A catalogue record for this book is available from the British Library

ISBN: 978-0-00-790212-5

Printed and bound in the UK using 100% renewable electricity at
CPI Group (UK) Ltd

MIX
Paper from
responsible sources
FSC™ C007454

FSC™ is a non-profit international organisation established to promote the
responsible management of the world's forests. Products carrying the FSC label
are independently certified to assure consumers that they come
from forests that are managed to meet the social, economic and
ecological needs of present and future generations.

Find out more about HarperCollins and the environment at
www.harpercollins.co.uk/green

Translated by George Fyler Townsend
Life & Times section © HarperCollins*Publishers* Ltd
Gerard Cheshire asserts his moral rights as author of the Life & Times section
Classic Literature: Words and Phrases adapted from
Collins English Dictionary
Typesetting in Kalix by Palimpsest Book Production Limited,
Falkirk, Stirlingshire

History of Collins

In 1819, millworker William Collins from Glasgow, Scotland, set up a company for printing and publishing pamphlets, sermons, hymn books and prayer books. That company was Collins and was to mark the birth of HarperCollins Publishers as we know it today. The long tradition of Collins dictionary publishing can be traced back to the first dictionary William published in 1824, *Greek and English Lexicon*. Indeed, from 1840 onwards, he began to produce illustrated dictionaries and even obtained a licence to print and publish the Bible.

Soon after, William published the first Collins novel, *Ready Reckoner*, however it was the time of the Long Depression, where harvests were poor, prices were high, potato crops had failed and violence was erupting in Europe. As a result, many factories across the country were forced to close down and William chose to retire in 1846, partly due to the hardships he was facing.

Aged 30, William's son, William II took over the business. A keen humanitarian with a warm heart and a generous spirit, William II was truly 'Victorian' in his outlook. He introduced new, up-to-date steam presses and published affordable editions of Shakespeare's works and *Pilgrim's Progress*, making them available to the masses for the first time. A new demand for educational books meant that success came with the publication of travel books, scientific books, encyclopaedias and dictionaries. This demand to be educated led to the later publication of atlases and Collins also held the monopoly on scripture writing at the time.

In the 1860s Collins began to expand and diversify

and the idea of 'books for the millions' was developed. Affordable editions of classical literature were published and in 1903 Collins introduced 10 titles in their Collins Handy Illustrated Pocket Novels. These proved so popular that a few years later this had increased to an output of 50 volumes, selling nearly half a million in their year of publication. In the same year, The Everyman's Library was also instituted, with the idea of publishing an affordable library of the most important classical works, biographies, religious and philosophical treatments, plays, poems, travel and adventure. This series eclipsed all competition at the time and the introduction of paperback books in the 1950s helped to open that market and marked a high point in the industry.

HarperCollins is and has always been a champion of the classics and the current Collins Classics series follows in this tradition—publishing classical literature that is affordable and available to all. Beautifully packaged, highly collectible and intended to be reread and enjoyed at every opportunity.

Life & Times

About the Author

Very little is known about Aesop and it is unclear as to whether he even existed – there are varying reports about his race and appearance. However, legend has it that he lived in Ancient Greece, circa 620–564 BC and that he was originally a slave who earned his freedom by imparting wisdom through his fables. He became revered as something of a generic folk hero to whom any tales of morality were attributed.

According to Ben Edwin Perry (1892–1968), who was the leading scholar on Aesop's fables, there are around 600 fables attributed to Aesop and listed in the Perry Index. The majority of listed fables are not well known, but a few have been popularized and continue to be retold by modern audiences. It seems inevitable that confusion often arises between Aesop's Fables, the stories of the Brothers Grimm, the Arabian Nights, and other traditional well-loved fairytales and proverbs as all often have strong moral undertones.

Aesop's fables typically feature talking and sometimes anthropomorphic animals in simple situations that impart a moral to the listener or reader. In many respects they are philosophical lessons of guidance and must originally have served the same purpose as the stories that were found in the Bible and other religious scriptures, only without the spiritual aspect.

The Fables

One of the best known fables in Aesop's collection is *The Hare and the Tortoise* in which, despite being a slower mover, a tortoise wins a race against a hare simply by pacing himself. The hare tires himself out by racing along at the start and is then arrogant enough to decide that he can have a sleep. Meanwhile the plodding tortoise creeps along at a steady rate, overtaking the sleeping hare and reaching the finishing line first.

Another classic fable is *The Shepherd's Boy and the Wolf*. A shepherd boy decides to play a practical joke by pretending that a wolf has come to kill his flock of sheep. The joke wears thin on the villagers who come to help each time he cries, 'wolf!' and they ultimately don't believe him or rush to his rescue when the wolf really does come and attack his flock.

In *The Crow and the Pitcher* a crow works out how to drink the water in a pitcher using his own ingenuity. Having attempted to tip the pitcher to one side he eventually realizes that the water will rise to the top if he drops pebbles into the pitcher and is rewarded with a drink.

The Fox and the Grapes tells of a fox attempting to reach a bunch of grapes hanging from a vine. After several failed attempts to get the grapes he announces that they are probably sour anyway and walks away. His pride will not allow him to lose face at failing to secure the grapes, so he makes the dissonant jibe not realizing that he has made more of a fool of himself by saying it.

The four fables outlined above serve to illustrate that there are many components to wisdom or sapience. The Ancient Greek culture was very serious about philosophical wisdom because it was seen as the quality that separated the civilized from the barbarian. Those within Greek society who lacked wisdom were despised as fools, so the teachings of fabulists were an essential part of educating the population. Similarly, barbarian slaves who displayed wisdom were able to earn their place in Greek society.

Very few of Aesop's fables involve human characters, partly perhaps because such fables were originally intended for the ears of children who might find stories told through humanized animals more engaging. The psychology of semiotics suggests that the use of animals helps the human mind to remember and distinguish characters. For example, if the tortoise and the hare were replaced by a patient man and a hasty man then the story would immediately lack the ingredients that make it stick in the mind, ensuring that the moral is delivered.

One of the few fables featuring a human character is *The Spendthrift and the Swallow*. A young man has squandered most of his possessions to satisfy his gambling addiction. All he has left is his coat, but when he sees a swallow he decides that summer has arrived and duly loses his coat on one last bet. Unfortunately the swallow is an early arrival and a spring frost kills the bird, whom the young man blames for his misfortune and discomfort. It would seem that there is a connection between this fable and the Aristotelian quote, 'One swallow does not a summer make, nor one fine day; similarly one day or brief time of happiness does not make a person entirely happy.' Whether a coincidence or influenced by Aesop's fable, the quote conveys a similar message – that foolhardy people make rash decisions and conclusions based on scant information, because their desires override their reasoning.

A similar fable is *The Hen and the Golden Eggs*. In this story a poor farmer is blessed with a hen able to lay golden eggs. However, his subsequent greed causes him to demand that the hen lays two golden eggs a day instead of just one. When the hen replies that it is not able to do so the farmer flies into a rage and kills the bird, destroying his salvation. Again, foolhardy action proves the undoing of the human character.

Part of the eternal appeal of Aesop's fables is the duality of what they offer. To the wise they are attractive because they cleverly relay established morals. To the unwise they are a revelation because they open up a world of simple wisdom that is easy to comprehend and digest. They make wonderful bedtime stories for children as they are brief to tell, yet serve to impart correct moral behaviour.

As Aesop's fables have been passed down through the generations they have proved quite mutable. Consequently, there are many different versions in existence because there are no original manuscripts from which to translate, although the essence of each fable remains intact. As each addressed moral requires a specific vehicle it has meant that the fables have indeed remained true to their ancient form, despite numerous alterations to the detail and length of the narrative. As fables were originally part of a storytelling tradition, people would have largely relied on their memory, rather than referring to written versions. Their mutability was therefore part of the equation and it gave the storyteller the opportunity to be intuitive about how to verbally edit the fables to best fit the situation in which the fables were being told.

AESOP'S
FABLES

CONTENTS

PREFACE

The Tale, the Parable, and the Fable are all common and popular modes of conveying instruction. Each is distinguished by its own special characteristics. The Tale consists simply in the narration of a story either founded on facts, or created solely by the imagination, and not necessarily associated with the teaching of any moral lesson. The Parable is the designed use of language purposely intended to convey a hidden and secret meaning other than that contained in the words themselves; and which may or may not bear a special reference to the hearer, or reader. The Fable partly agrees with, and partly differs from both of these. It will contain, like the Tale, a short but real narrative; it will seek, like the Parable, to convey a hidden meaning, and that not so much by the use of language, as by the skilful introduction of fictitious characters; and yet unlike to either Tale or Parable, it will ever keep in view, as its high prerogative, and inseparable attribute, the great purpose of instruction, and will necessarily seek to inculcate some moral maxim, social duty, or political truth. The true Fable, if it rises to its high requirements, ever aims at one great end and purpose representation of human motive, and the improvement of human conduct, and yet it so conceals its design under the disguise of fictitious characters, by

clothing with speech the animals of the field, the birds of the
air, the trees of the wood, or the beasts of the forest, that
the reader shall receive advice without perceiving the presence
of the adviser. Thus the superiority of the counsellor, which
often renders counsel unpalatable, is kept out of view, and
the lesson comes with the greater acceptance when the reader
is led, unconsciously to himself, to have his sympathies
enlisted on behalf of what is pure, honorable, and praise-
worthy, and to have his indignation excited against what is
low, ignoble, and unworthy. The true fabulist, therefore,
discharges a most important function. He is neither a narrator,
nor an allegorist. He is a great teacher, a corrector of morals,
a censor of vice, and a commender of virtue. In this consists
the superiority of the Fable over the Tale or the Parable. The
fabulist is to create a laugh, but yet, under a merry guise, to
convey instruction. Phaedrus, the great imitator of Aesop,
plainly indicates this double purpose to be the true office of
the writer of fables.

> Duplex libelli dos est: quod risum movet,
> Et quod prudenti vitam consilio monet.

The continual observance of this twofold aim creates the
charm, and accounts for the universal favor, of the fables of
Aesop. "The fable", says Professor K. O. Mueller, "originated
in Greece in an intentional travestie of human affairs. The
'ainos', as its name denotes, is an admonition, or rather a
reproof veiled, either from fear of an excess of frankness, or
from a love of fun and jest, beneath the fiction of an occur-
rence happening among beasts; and wherever we have any
ancient and authentic account of the Aesopian fables, we find
it to be the same."

The construction of a fable involves a minute attention
to (1) the narration itself; (2) the deduction of the moral; and
(3) a careful maintenance of the individual characteristics of

the fictitious personages introduced into it. The narration should relate to one simple action, consistent with itself, and neither be overladen with a multiplicity of details, nor distracted by a variety of circumstances. The moral or lesson should be so plain, and so intimately interwoven with, and so necessarily dependent on, the narration, that every reader should be compelled to give to it the same undeniable interpretation. The introduction of the animals or fictitious characters should be marked with an unexceptionable care and attention to their natural attributes, and to the qualities attributed to them by universal popular consent. The Fox should be always cunning, the Hare timid, the Lion bold, the Wolf cruel, the Bull strong, the Horse proud, and the Ass patient. Many of these fables are characterized by the strictest observance of these rules. They are occupied with one short narrative, from which the moral naturally flows, and with which it is intimately associated. "'Tis the simple manner," says Dodsley, "in which the morals of Aesop are interwoven with his fables that distinguishes him, and gives him the preference over all other mythologists. His 'Mountain delivered of a Mouse', produces the moral of his fable in ridicule of pompous pretenders; and his Crow, when she drops her cheese, lets fall, as it were by accident, the strongest admonition against the power of flattery. There is no need of a separate sentence to explain it; no possibility of impressing it deeper, by that load we too often see of accumulated reflections." An equal amount of praise is due for the consistency with which the characters of the animals, fictitiously introduced, are marked. While they are made to depict the motives and passions of men, they retain, in an eminent degree, their own special features of craft or counsel, of cowardice or courage, of generosity or rapacity.

These terms of praise, it must be confessed, cannot be bestowed on all the fables in this collection. Many of them lack that unity of design, that close connection of the moral with the narrative, that wise choice in the introduction of the animals, which constitute the charm and excellency of true Aesopian fable. This inferiority of some to others is sufficiently accounted for in the history of the origin and descent of these fables. The great bulk of them are not the immediate work of Aesop. Many are obtained from ancient authors prior to the time in which he lived. Thus, the fable of the "Hawk and the Nightingale" is related by Hesiod; the "Eagle wounded by an Arrow, winged with its own Feathers", by Aeschylus; the "Fox avenging his wrongs on the Eagle", by Archilochus. Many of them again are of later origin, and are to be traced to the monks of the middle ages: and yet this collection, though thus made up of fables both earlier and later than the era of Aesop, rightfully bears his name, because he composed so large a number (all framed in the same mould, and conformed to the same fashion, and stamped with the same lineaments, image, and superscription) as to secure to himself the right to be considered the father of Greek fables, and the founder of this class of writing, which has ever since borne his name, and has secured for him, through all succeeding ages, the position of the first of moralists.

The fables were in the first instance only narrated by Aesop, and for a long time were handed down by the uncertain channel of oral tradition. Socrates is mentioned by Plato as having employed his time while in prison, awaiting the return of the sacred ship from Delphos which was to be the signal of his death, in turning some of these fables into verse, but he thus versified only such as he remembered. Demetrius Phalereus, a philosopher at Athens about 300 B.C., is said to have made the first collection of these fables. Phaedrus, a slave by birth or by subsequent misfortunes, and admitted by Augustus to the honors of a freedman, imitated many of these fables in Latin iambics about the commencement of the Christian era. Aphthonius, a rhetorician of Antioch, A.D. 315, wrote a treatise on, and converted into Latin prose, some of these fables. This translation is the more worthy of notice, as it illustrates a custom of common use, both in these and in later times. The rhetoricians and philosophers were accustomed to give the Fables of Aesop as an exercise to their scholars, not only inviting them to discuss the moral of the tale, but also to practice and to perfect themselves thereby in style and rules of grammar, by making for themselves new and various versions of the fables. Ausonius, the friend of the Emperor Valentinian, and the latest poet of eminence in the Western Empire, has handed down some of these fables in verse, which Julianus Titianus, a contemporary writer of no great name, translated into prose. Avienus, also a contemporary of Ausonius, put some of these fables into Latin elegiacs, which are given by Nevelet (in a book we shall refer to hereafter), and are occasionally incorporated with the editions of Phaedrus.

Seven centuries elapsed before the next notice is found of the Fables of Aesop. During this long period these fables seem to have suffered an eclipse, to have disappeared and to have been forgotten; and it is at the commencement of the fourteenth century, when the Byzantine emperors were the great patrons of learning, and amidst the splendors of an Asiatic court, that we next find honors paid to the name and memory of Aesop. Maximus Planudes, a learned monk of Constantinople, made a collection of about a hundred and fifty of these fables. Little is known of his history. Planudes, however, was no mere recluse, shut up in his monastery. He took an active part in public affairs. In 1327 A.D. he was sent on a diplomatic mission to Venice by the Emperor Andronicus the Elder. This brought him into immediate contact with the Western Patriarch, whose interests he henceforth advocated with so much zeal as to bring on him suspicion and persecution from the rulers of the Eastern Church. Planudes has been exposed to a two-fold accusation. He is charged on the one hand with having had before him a copy of Babrias (to whom we shall have occasion to refer at greater length in the end of this Preface), and to have had the bad taste "to transpose", or to turn his poetical version into prose: and he is asserted, on the other hand, never to have seen the Fables of Aesop at all, but to have himself invented and made the fables which he palmed off under the name of the famous Greek fabulist. The truth lies between these two extremes. Planudes may have invented some few fables, or have inserted some that were current in his day; but there is an abundance of unanswerable internal evidence to prove that he had an acquaintance with the veritable fables of Aesop, although the versions he had access to were probably corrupt, as contained in the various translations and disquisitional exercises of the rhetoricians and philosophers. His collection is interesting and important, not only as the parent source or foundation of the earlier printed versions of Aesop, but as the direct channel of attracting to these fables the attention of the learned.

The eventual re-introduction, however, of these Fables of Aesop to their high place in the general literature of Christendom, is to be looked for in the West rather than in the East. The calamities gradually thickening round the Eastern Empire, and the fall of Constantinople, 1453 A.D. combined with other events to promote the rapid restoration of learning in Italy; and with that recovery of learning the revival of an interest in the Fables of Aesop is closely identified. These fables, indeed, were among the first writings of an earlier antiquity that attracted attention. They took their place beside the Holy Scriptures and the ancient classic authors, in the minds of the great students of that day. Lorenzo Valla, one of the most famous promoters of Italian learning, not only translated into Latin the Iliad of Homer and the Histories of Herodotus and Thucydides, but also the Fables of Aesop.

These fables, again, were among the books brought into an extended circulation by the agency of the printing press.

Bonus Accursius, as early as 1475-1480, printed the collection of these fables, made by Planudes, which, within five years afterwards, Caxton translated into English, and printed at his press in Westminster Abbey, 1485. It must be mentioned also that the learning of this age has left permanent traces of its influence on these fables, by causing the interpolation with them of some of those amusing stories which were so frequently introduced into the public discourses of the great preachers of those days, and of which specimens are yet to be found in the extant sermons of Jean Raulin, Meffreth, and Gabriel Barlette. The publication of this era which most probably has influenced these fables, is the "Liber Facetiarum", a book consisting of a hundred jests and stories, by the celebrated Poggio Bracciolini, published A.D. 1471, from which the two fables of the "Miller, his Son, and the Ass", and the "Fox and the Woodcutter", are undoubtedly selected.

The knowledge of these fables rapidly spread from Italy into Germany, and their popularity was increased by the favor and sanction given to them by the great fathers of the Reformation, who frequently used them as vehicles for satire and protest against the tricks and abuses of the Romish ecclesiastics. The zealous and renowned Camerarius, who took an active part in the preparation of the Confession of Augsburgh, found time, amidst his numerous avocations, to prepare a version for the students in the university of Tubingen, in which he was a professor. Martin Luther translated twenty of these fables, and was urged by Melancthon to complete the whole; while Gottfried Arnold, the celebrated Lutheran theologian, and librarian to Frederick I, king of Prussia, mentions that the great Reformer valued the Fables of Aesop next after the Holy Scriptures. In 1546 A.D. the second printed edition of the collection of the Fables made by Planudes, was issued from the printing-press of Robert Stephens, in which were inserted some additional fables from an MS. in the Bibliotheque du Roy at Paris.

The greatest advance, however, towards a re-introduction of the Fables of Aesop to a place in the literature of the world, was made in the early part of the seventeenth century. In the year 1610, a learned Swiss, Isaac Nicholas Nevelet, sent forth the third printed edition of these fables, in a work entitled "Mythologia Aesopica". This was a noble effort to do honor to the great fabulist, and was the most perfect collection of Aesopian fables ever yet published. It consisted, in addition to the collection of fables given by Planudes and reprinted in the various earlier editions, of one hundred and thirty-six new fables (never before published) from MSS. in the Library of the Vatican, of forty fables attributed to Aphthonius, and of forty-three from Babrias. It also contained the Latin versions of the same fables by Phaedrus, Avienus, and other authors. This volume of Nevelet forms a complete "Corpus Fabularum Aesopicarum"; and to his labors Aesop owes his restoration to universal favor as one of the wise moralists and great teachers of mankind. During the interval of three centuries which has elapsed since the publication of this volume of Nevelet's, no book, with the exception of the Holy Scriptures, has had a wider circulation than Aesop's Fables. They have been translated into the greater number of the languages both of Europe and of the East, and have been read, and will be read, for generations, alike by Jew, Heathen, Mohammedan, and Christian. They are, at the present time, not only engrafted into the literature of the civilized world, but are familiar as household words in the common intercourse and daily conversation of the inhabitants of all countries.

This collection of Nevelet's is the great culminating point in the history of the revival of the fame and reputation of Aesopian Fables. It is remarkable, also, as containing in its preface the germ of an idea, which has been since proved to have been correct by a strange chain of circumstances. Nevelet intimates an opinion, that a writer named Babrias would be found to be the veritable author of the existing form of

Aesopian Fables. This intimation has since given rise to a series of inquiries, the knowledge of which is necessary, in the present day, to a full understanding of the true position of Aesop in connection with the writings that bear his name.

The history of Babrias is so strange and interesting, that it might not unfitly be enumerated among the curiosities of literature. He is generally supposed to have been a Greek of Asia Minor, of one of the Ionic Colonies, but the exact period in which he lived and wrote is yet unsettled. He is placed, by one critic, as far back as the institution of the Achaian League, B.C. 250; by another as late as the Emperor Severus, who died A.D. 235; while others make him a contemporary with Phaedrus in the time of Augustus. At whatever time he wrote his version of Aesop, by some strange accident it seems to have entirely disappeared, and to have been lost sight of. His name is mentioned by Avienus; by Suidas, a celebrated critic, at the close of the eleventh century, who gives in his lexicon several isolated verses of his version of the fables; and by John Tzetzes, a grammarian and poet of Constantinople, who lived during the latter half of the twelfth century. Nevelet, in the preface to the volume which we have described, points out that the Fables of Planudes could not be the work of Aesop, as they contain a reference in two places to "Holy monks", and give a verse from the Epistle of St. James as an "Epimith" to one of the fables, and suggests Babrias as their author. Francis Vavassor, a learned French jesuit, entered at greater length on this subject, and produced further proofs from internal evidence, from the use of the word Piraeus in describing the harbour of Athens, a name which was not given till two hundred years after Aesop, and from the introduction of other modern words, that many of these fables must have been at least committed to writing posterior to the time of Aesop, and more boldly suggests Babrias as their author or collector. These various references to Babrias induced Dr. Plichard Bentley, at the close of the seventeenth century, to examine more minutely the existing versions of Aesop's Fables, and he maintained that many of them could, with a slight change of words, be resolved into the Scazonic iambics, in which Babrias is known to have written: and, with a greater freedom than the evidence then justified, he put forth, in behalf of Babrias, a claim to the exclusive authorship of these fables. Such a seemingly extravagant theory, thus roundly asserted, excited much opposition. Dr. Bentley met with an able antagonist in a member of the University of Oxford, the Hon. Mr. Charles Boyle, afterwards Earl of Orrery. Their letters and disputations on this subject, enlivened on both sides with much wit and learning, will ever bear a conspicuous place in the literary history of the seventeenth century. The arguments of Dr. Bentley were yet further defended a few years later by Mr. Thomas Tyrwhitt, a well-read scholar, who gave up high civil distinctions that he might devote himself the more unreservedly to literary pursuits. Mr. Tyrwhitt published, A.D. 1776, a Dissertation on Babrias, and a collection of his fables in choliambic meter found in a MS. in the Bodleian Library at Oxford. Francesco de Furia, a learned Italian, contributed further testimony to the correctness of the supposition that Babrias had made a veritable collection of fables by printing from a MS. contained in the Vatican library several fables never before published. In the year 1844, however, new and unexpected light was thrown upon this subject. A veritable copy of Babrias was found in a manner as singular as were the MSS. of Quinctilian's Institutes, and of Cicero's Orations by Poggio in the monastery of St. Gall A.D. 1416. M. Menoides, at the suggestion of M. Villemain, Minister of Public Instruction to King Louis Philippe, had been entrusted with a commission to search for ancient MSS., and in carrying out his instructions he found a MS. at the convent of St. Laura, on Mount Athos, which proved to be a copy of the long suspected and wished-for choliambic version of Babrias. This MS. was found to be divided into two books, the one containing a hundred and twenty-five, and the other ninety-five fables. This discovery attracted very general attention, not only as confirming, in a singular manner, the conjectures so boldly made by a long chain of critics, but as bringing to light valuable literary treasures tending to establish the reputation, and to confirm the antiquity and authenticity of the great mass of Aesopian Fable. The Fables thus recovered were soon published. They found a most worthy editor in the late distinguished Sir George Cornewall Lewis, and a translator equally qualified for his task, in the Reverend James Davies, M.A., sometime a scholar of Lincoln College, Oxford, and himself a relation of their English editor. Thus, after an eclipse of many centuries, Babrias shines out as the earliest, and most reliable collector of veritable Aesopian Fables.

THE WOLF AND THE LAMB

Wolf, meeting with a Lamb astray from the fold, resolved not to lay violent hands on him, but to find some plea to justify to the Lamb the Wolf's right to eat him. He thus addressed him: "Sirrah, last year you grossly insulted me." "Indeed," bleated the Lamb in a mournful tone of voice, "I was not then born." Then said the Wolf, "You feed in my pasture." "No, good sir," replied the Lamb, "I have not yet tasted grass." Again said the Wolf, "You drink of my well." "No," exclaimed the Lamb, "I never yet drank water, for as yet my mother's milk is both food and drink to me." Upon which the Wolf seized him and ate him up, saying, "Well! I won't remain supperless, even though you refute every one of my imputations." The tyrant will always find a pretext for his tyranny.

THE BAT AND THE WEASELS

A Bat who fell upon the ground and was caught by a Weasel pleaded to be spared his life. The Weasel refused, saying that he was by nature the enemy of all birds. The Bat assured him that he was not a bird, but a mouse, and thus was set free. Shortly afterwards the Bat again fell to the ground and was caught by another Weasel, whom he likewise entreated not to eat him. The Weasel said that he had a special hostility to mice. The Bat assured him that he was not a mouse, but a bat, and thus a second time escaped.

It is wise to turn circumstances to good account.

THE ASS AND
THE GRASSHOPPER

An Ass having heard some Grasshoppers chirping, was highly enchanted; and, desiring to possess the same charms of melody, demanded what sort of food they lived on to give them such beautiful voices. They replied, "The dew." The Ass resolved that he would live only upon dew, and in a short time died of hunger.

THE LION AND THE MOUSE

A Lion was awakened from sleep by a Mouse running over his face. Rising up angrily, he caught him and was about to kill him, when the Mouse piteously entreated, saying: "If you would only spare my life, I would be sure to repay your kindness." The Lion laughed and let him go. It happened shortly after this that the Lion was caught by some hunters, who bound him by strong ropes to the ground. The Mouse, recognizing his roar, came and gnawed the rope with his teeth, and set him free, exclaiming:

"You ridiculed the idea of my ever being able to help you, not expecting to receive from me any repayment of your favor; now you know that it is possible for even a Mouse to confer benefits on a Lion."

THE CHARCOAL-BURNER
AND THE FULLER

A Charcoal-burner carried on his trade in his own house. One day he met a friend, a Fuller, and entreated him to come and live with him, saying that they should be far better neighbors and that their housekeeping expenses would be lessened. The Fuller replied, "The arrangement is impossible as far as I am concerned, for whatever I should whiten, you would immediately blacken again with your charcoal."

Like will draw like.

THE FATHER AND HIS SONS

A Father had a family of sons who were perpetually quarreling among themselves. When he failed to heal their disputes by his exhortations, he determined to give them a practical illustration of the evils of disunion; and for this purpose he one day told them to bring him a bundle of sticks. When they had done so, he placed the faggot into the hands of each of them in succession, and ordered them to break it in pieces. They tried with all their strength, and were not able to do it. He next opened the faggot, took the sticks separately, one by one, and again put them into his sons' hands, upon which they broke them easily. He then addressed them in these words: "My sons, if you are of one mind, and unite to assist each other, you will be as this faggot, uninjured by all the attempts of your enemies; but if you are divided among yourselves, you will be broken as easily as these sticks."

THE BOY HUNTING LOCUSTS

A Boy was hunting for locusts. He had caught a goodly number, when he saw a Scorpion, and mistaking him for a locust, reached out his hand to take him. The Scorpion, showing his sting, said: "If you had but touched me, my friend, you would have lost me, and all your locusts too!"

THE COCK AND THE JEWEL

A Cock, scratching for food for himself and his hens, found a precious stone and exclaimed: "If your owner had found thee, and not I, he would have taken thee up, and have set thee in thy first estate; but I have found thee for no purpose. I would rather have one barleycorn than all the jewels in the world."

THE KINGDOM OF THE LION

The Beasts of the field and forest had a Lion as their king. He was neither wrathful, cruel, nor tyrannical, but just and gentle as a king could be. During his reign he made a royal proclamation for a general assembly of all the birds and beasts, and drew up conditions for a universal league, in which the Wolf and the Lamb, the Panther and the Kid, the Tiger and the Stag, the Dog and the Hare, should live together in perfect peace and amity. The Hare said, "Oh, how I have longed to see this day, in which the weak shall take their place with impunity by the side of the strong." And after the Hare said this, he ran for his life.

THE WOLF AND THE CRANE

A Wolf who had a bone stuck in his throat hired a Crane, for a large sum, to put her head into his mouth and draw out the bone. When the Crane had extracted the bone and demanded the promised payment, the Wolf, grinning and grinding his teeth, exclaimed: "Why, you have surely already had a sufficient recompense, in having been permitted to draw out your head in safety from the mouth and jaws of a wolf."

In serving the wicked, expect no reward, and be thankful if you escape injury for your pains.

THE FISHERMAN PIPING

A Fisherman skilled in music took his flute and his nets to the seashore. Standing on a projecting rock, he played several tunes in the hope that the fish, attracted by his melody, would of their own accord dance into his net, which he had placed below. At last, having long waited in vain, he laid aside his flute, and casting his net into the sea, made an excellent haul of fish. When he saw them leaping about in the net upon the rock he said: "O you most perverse creatures, when I piped you would not dance, but now that I have ceased you do so merrily."

HERCULES AND
THE WAGONER

A Carter was driving a wagon along a country lane, when the wheels sank down deep into a rut. The rustic driver, stupefied and aghast, stood looking at the wagon, and did nothing but utter loud cries to Hercules to come and help him. Hercules, it is said, appeared and thus addressed him: "Put your shoulders to the wheels, my man. Goad on your bullocks, and never more pray to me for help, until you have done your best to help yourself, or depend upon it you will henceforth pray in vain."

Self-help is the best help.

THE ANTS AND
THE GRASSHOPPER

The Ants were spending a fine winter's day drying grain collected in the summertime. A Grasshopper, perishing with famine, passed by and earnestly begged for a little food. The Ants inquired of him, "Why did you not treasure up food during the summer?" He replied, "I had not leisure enough. I passed the days in singing." They then said in derision: "If you were foolish enough to sing all the summer, you must dance supperless to bed in the winter."

THE TRAVELER AND HIS DOG

A Traveler about to set out on a journey saw his Dog stand at the door stretching himself. He asked him sharply: "Why do you stand there gaping? Everything is ready but you, so come with me instantly." The Dog, wagging his tail, replied: "O, master! I am quite ready; it is you for whom I am waiting." The loiterer often blames delay on his more active friend.

THE DOG AND THE SHADOW

A Dog, crossing a bridge over a stream with a piece of flesh in his mouth, saw his own shadow in the water and took it for that of another Dog, with a piece of meat double his own in size. He immediately let go of his own, and fiercely attacked the other Dog to get his larger piece from him. He thus lost both: that which he grasped at in the water, because it was a shadow; and his own, because the stream swept it away.

THE MOLE AND HIS MOTHER

A Mole, a creature blind from birth, once said to his Mother: "I am sure than I can see, Mother!" In the desire to prove to him his mistake, his Mother placed before him a few grains of frankincense, and asked, "What is it?" The young Mole said, "It is a pebble." His Mother exclaimed: "My son, I am afraid that you are not only blind, but that you have lost your sense of smell."

THE HERDSMAN AND
THE LOST BULL

A Herdsman tending his flock in a forest lost a Bull-calf from the fold. After a long and fruitless search, he made a vow that, if he could only discover the thief who had stolen the Calf, he would offer a lamb in sacrifice to Hermes, Pan, and the Guardian Deities of the forest. Not long afterwards, as he ascended a small hillock, he saw at its foot a Lion feeding on the Calf. Terrified at the sight, he lifted his eyes and his hands to heaven, and said: "Just now I vowed to offer a lamb to the Guardian Deities of the forest if I could only find out who had robbed me; but now that I have discovered the thief, I would willingly add a full-grown Bull to the Calf I have lost, if I may only secure my own escape from him in safety."

THE HARE AND
THE TORTOISE

A Hare one day ridiculed the short feet and slow pace of the Tortoise, who replied, laughing: "Though you be swift as the wind, I will beat you in a race." The Hare, believing her assertion to be simply impossible, assented to the proposal; and they agreed that the Fox should choose the course and fix the goal. On the day appointed for the race the two started together. The Tortoise never for a moment stopped, but went on with a slow but steady pace straight to the end of the course. The Hare, lying down by the wayside, fell fast asleep. At last waking up, and moving as fast as he could, he saw the Tortoise had reached the goal, and was comfortably dozing after her fatigue.

Slow but steady wins the race.

THE POMEGRANATE,
APPLE-TREE, AND BRAMBLE

The Pomegranate and Apple-Tree disputed as to which was the most beautiful. When their strife was at its height, a Bramble from the neighboring hedge lifted up its voice, and said in a boastful tone: "Pray, my dear friends, in my presence at least cease from such vain disputings."

THE FARMER AND
THE STORK

A Farmer placed nets on his newly-sown plowlands and caught a number of Cranes, which came to pick up his seed. With them he trapped a Stork that had fractured his leg in the net and was earnestly beseeching the Farmer to spare his life. "Pray save me, Master," he said, "and let me go free this once. My broken limb should excite your pity. Besides, I am no Crane, I am a Stork, a bird of excellent character; and see how I love and slave for my father and mother. Look too, at my feathers—they are not the least like those of a Crane." The Farmer laughed aloud and said, "It may be all as you say, I only know this: I have taken you with these robbers, the Cranes, and you must die in their company."

Birds of a feather flock together.

THE FARMER AND
THE SNAKE

One winter a Farmer found a Snake stiff and frozen with cold. He had compassion on it, and taking it up, placed it in his bosom. The Snake was quickly revived by the warmth, and resuming its natural instincts, bit its benefactor, inflicting on him a mortal wound. "Oh," cried the Farmer with his last breath, "I am rightly served for pitying a scoundrel."

The greatest kindness will not bind the ungrateful.

THE FAWN AND
HIS MOTHER

A young Fawn once said to his Mother, "You are larger than a dog, and swifter, and more used to running, and you have your horns as a defense; why, then, O Mother! do the hounds frighten you so?" She smiled, and said: "I know full well, my son, that all you say is true. I have the advantages you mention, but when I hear even the bark of a single dog I feel ready to faint, and fly away as fast as I can."

No arguments will give courage to the coward.

THE BEAR AND THE FOX

A Bear boasted very much of his philanthropy, saying that of all animals he was the most tender in his regard for man, for he had such respect for him that he would not even touch his dead body. A Fox hearing these words said with a smile to the Bear, "Oh! that you would eat the dead and not the living."

THE SWALLOW AND
THE CROW

The Swallow and the Crow had a contention about their plumage. The Crow put an end to the dispute by saying, "Your feathers are all very well in the spring, but mine protect me against the winter."

Fair weather friends are not worth much.

THE MOUNTAIN IN LABOR

A Mountain was once greatly agitated. Loud groans and noises were heard, and crowds of people came from all parts to see what was the matter. While they were assembled in anxious expectation of some terrible calamity, out came a Mouse.

Don't make much ado about nothing.

THE ASS, THE FOX,
AND THE LION

The Ass and the Fox, having entered into partnership together for their mutual protection, went out into the forest to hunt. They had not proceeded far when they met a Lion. The Fox, seeing imminent danger, approached the Lion and promised to contrive for him the capture of the Ass if the Lion would pledge his word not to harm the Fox. Then, upon assuring the Ass that he would not be injured, the Fox led him to a deep pit and arranged that he should fall into it. The Lion, seeing that the Ass was secured, immediately clutched the Fox, and attacked the Ass at his leisure.

THE TORTOISE AND
THE EAGLE

A Tortoise, lazily basking in the sun, complained to the sea-birds of her hard fate, that no one would teach her to fly. An Eagle, hovering near, heard her lamentation and demanded what reward she would give him if he would take her aloft and float her in the air. "I will give you," she said, "all the riches of the Red Sea." "I will teach you to fly then," said the Eagle; and taking her up in his talons he carried her almost to the clouds suddenly he let her go, and she fell on a lofty mountain, dashing her shell to pieces. The Tortoise exclaimed in the moment of death: "I have deserved my present fate; for what had I to do with wings and clouds, who can with difficulty move about on the earth?"

If men had all they wished, they would be often ruined.

THE FLIES AND
THE HONEY-POT

A number of Flies were attracted to a jar of honey which had been overturned in a housekeeper's room, and placing their feet in it, ate greedily. Their feet, however, became so smeared with the honey that they could not use their wings, nor release themselves, and were suffocated. Just as they were expiring, they exclaimed, "O foolish creatures that we are, for the sake of a little pleasure we have destroyed ourselves."

Pleasure bought with pains, hurts.

THE MAN AND THE LION

A Man and a Lion traveled together through the forest. They soon began to boast of their respective superiority to each other in strength and prowess. As they were disputing, they passed a statue carved in stone, which represented "a Lion strangled by a Man." The traveler pointed to it and said: "See there! How strong we are, and how we prevail over even the king of beasts." The Lion replied: "This statue was made by one of you Men. If we Lions knew how to erect statues, you would see the Man placed under the paw of the Lion."

One story is good, till another is told.

THE FARMER AND
THE CRANES

Some Cranes made their feeding grounds on some plowlands newly sown with wheat. For a long time the Farmer, brandishing an empty sling, chased them away by the terror he inspired; but when the birds found that the sling was only swung in the air, they ceased to take any notice of it and would not move. The Farmer, on seeing this, charged his sling with stones, and killed a great number. The remaining birds at once forsook his fields, crying to each other, "It is time for us to be off to Liliput: for this man is no longer content to scare us, but begins to show us in earnest what he can do."

If words suffice not, blows must follow.

THE DOG IN THE MANGER

A Dog lay in a manger, and by his growling and snapping prevented the oxen from eating the hay which had been placed for them. "What a selfish Dog!" said one of them to his companions; "he cannot eat the hay himself, and yet refuses to allow those to eat who can."

THE FOX AND THE GOAT

A Fox one day fell into a deep well and could find no means of escape. A Goat, overcome with thirst, came to the same well, and seeing the Fox, inquired if the water was good. Concealing his sad plight under a merry guise, the Fox indulged in a lavish praise of the water, saying it was excellent beyond measure, and encouraging him to descend. The Goat, mindful only of his thirst, thoughtlessly jumped down, but just as he drank, the Fox informed him of the difficulty they were both in and suggested a scheme for their common escape. "If," said he, "you will place your forefeet upon the wall and bend your head, I will run up your back and escape, and will help you out afterwards." The Goat readily assented and the Fox leaped upon his back. Steadying himself with the Goat's horns, he safely reached the mouth of the well and made off as fast as he could. When the Goat upbraided him for breaking his promise, he turned around and cried out, "You foolish old fellow! If you had as many brains in your head as you have hairs in your beard, you would never have gone down before you had inspected the way up, nor have exposed yourself to dangers from which you had no means of escape."

Look before you leap.

THE BEAR AND
THE TWO TRAVELERS

Two Men were traveling together, when a Bear suddenly met them on their path. One of them climbed up quickly into a tree and concealed himself in the branches. The other, seeing that he must be attacked, fell flat on the ground, and when the Bear came up and felt him with his snout, and smelt him all over, he held his breath, and feigned the appearance of death as much as he could. The Bear soon left him, for it is said he will not touch a dead body. When he was quite gone, the other Traveler descended from the tree, and jocularly inquired of his friend what it was the Bear had whispered in his ear. "He gave me this advice," his companion replied. "Never travel with a friend who deserts you at the approach of danger."

Misfortune tests the sincerity of friends.

THE OXEN AND
THE AXLE-TREES

A heavy wagon was being dragged along a country lane by a team of Oxen. The Axle-trees groaned and creaked terribly; whereupon the Oxen, turning round, thus addressed the wheels: "Hullo there! why do you make so much noise? We bear all the labor, and we, not you, ought to cry out."

Those who suffer most cry out the least.

THE THIRSTY PIGEON

A Pigeon, oppressed by excessive thirst, saw a goblet of water painted on a signboard. Not supposing it to be only a picture, she flew towards it with a loud whir and unwittingly dashed against the signboard, jarring herself terribly. Having broken her wings by the blow, she fell to the ground, and was caught by one of the bystanders.

Zeal should not outrun discretion.

THE RAVEN AND THE SWAN

A Raven saw a Swan and desired to secure for himself the same beautiful plumage. Supposing that the Swan's splendid white color arose from his washing in the water in which he swam, the Raven left the altars in the neighborhood where he picked up his living, and took up residence in the lakes and pools. But cleansing his feathers as often as he would, he could not change their color, while through want of food he perished.

Change of habit cannot alter Nature.

THE GOAT AND
THE GOATHERD

A Goatherd had sought to bring back a stray goat to his flock. He whistled and sounded his horn in vain; the straggler paid no attention to the summons. At last the Goatherd threw a stone, and breaking its horn, begged the Goat not to tell his master. The Goat replied, "Why, you silly fellow, the horn will speak though I be silent."

Do not attempt to hide things which cannot be hid.

THE MISER

A Miser sold all that he had and bought a lump of gold, which he buried in a hole in the ground by the side of an old wall and went to look at daily. One of his workmen observed his frequent visits to the spot and decided to watch his movements. He soon discovered the secret of the hidden treasure, and digging down, came to the lump of gold, and stole it. The Miser, on his next visit, found the hole empty and began to tear his hair and to make loud lamentations. A neighbor, seeing him overcome with grief and learning the cause, said, "Pray do not grieve so; but go and take a stone, and place it in the hole, and fancy that the gold is still lying there. It will do you quite the same service; for when the gold was there, you had it not, as you did not make the slightest use of it."

THE SICK LION

A Lion, unable from old age and infirmities to provide himself with food by force, resolved to do so by artifice. He returned to his den, and lying down there, pretended to be sick, taking care that his sickness should be publicly known. The beasts expressed their sorrow, and came one by one to his den, where the Lion devoured them. After many of the beasts had thus disappeared, the Fox discovered the trick and presenting himself to the Lion, stood on the outside of the cave, at a respectful distance, and asked him how he was. "I am very middling," replied the Lion, "but why do you stand without? Pray enter within to talk with me." "No, thank you," said the Fox. "I notice that there are many prints of feet entering your cave, but I see no trace of any returning."

He is wise who is warned by the misfortunes of others.

THE HORSE AND GROOM

A Groom used to spend whole days in currycombing and rubbing down his Horse, but at the same time stole his oats and sold them for his own profit. "Alas!" said the Horse, "if you really wish me to be in good condition, you should groom me less, and feed me more."

THE ASS AND THE LAPDOG

A man had an Ass, and a Maltese Lapdog, a very great beauty. The Ass was left in a stable and had plenty of oats and hay to eat, just as any other Ass would. The Lapdog knew many tricks and was a great favorite with his master, who often fondled him and seldom went out to dine without bringing him home some tidbit to eat. The Ass, on the contrary, had much work to do in grinding the corn-mill and in carrying wood from the forest or burdens from the farm. He often lamented his own hard fate and contrasted it with the luxury and idleness of the Lapdog, till at last one day he broke his cords and halter, and galloped into his master's house, kicking up his heels without measure, and frisking and fawning as well as he could. He next tried to jump about his master as he had seen the Lapdog do, but he broke the table and smashed all the dishes upon it to atoms. He then attempted to lick his master, and jumped upon his back. The servants, hearing the strange hubbub and perceiving the danger of their master, quickly relieved him, and drove out the Ass to his stable with kicks and clubs and cuffs. The Ass, as he returned to his stall beaten nearly to death, thus lamented: "I have brought it all on myself! Why could I not have been contented to labor with my companions, and not wish to be idle all the day like that useless little Lapdog!"

THE LIONESS

A controversy prevailed among the beasts of the field as to which of the animals deserved the most credit for producing the greatest number of whelps at a birth. They rushed clamorously into the presence of the Lioness and demanded of her the settlement of the dispute. "And you," they said, "how many sons have you at a birth?" The Lioness laughed at them, and said: "Why! I have only one; but that one is altogether a thoroughbred Lion."

The value is in the worth, not in the number.

THE BOASTING TRAVELER

A man who had traveled in foreign lands boasted very much, on returning to his own country, of the many wonderful and heroic feats he had performed in the different places he had visited. Among other things, he said that when he was at Rhodes he had leaped to such a distance that no man of his day could leap anywhere near him as to that, there were in Rhodes many persons who saw him do it and whom he could call as witnesses. One of the bystanders interrupted him, saying: "Now, my good man, if this be all true there is no need of witnesses. Suppose this to be Rhodes, and leap for us."

THE CAT AND THE COCK

A Cat caught a Cock, and pondered how he might find a reasonable excuse for eating him. He accused him of being a nuisance to men by crowing in the nighttime and not permitting them to sleep. The Cock defended himself by saying that he did this for the benefit of men, that they might rise in time for their labors. The Cat replied, "Although you abound in specious apologies, I shall not remain supperless;" and he made a meal of him.

THE PIGLET, THE SHEEP, AND THE GOAT

A young Pig was shut up in a fold-yard with a Goat and a Sheep. On one occasion when the shepherd laid hold of him, he grunted and squeaked and resisted violently. The Sheep and the Goat complained of his distressing cries, saying, "He often handles us, and we do not cry out." To this the Pig replied, "Your handling and mine are very different things. He catches you only for your wool, or your milk, but he lays hold on me for my very life."

THE BOY AND
THE FILBERTS

A Boy put his hand into a pitcher full of filberts. He grasped as many as he could possibly hold, but when he tried to pull out his hand, he was prevented from doing so by the neck of the pitcher. Unwilling to lose his filberts, and yet unable to withdraw his hand, he burst into tears and bitterly lamented his disappointment. A bystander said to him, "Be satisfied with half the quantity, and you will readily draw out your hand."

Do not attempt too much at once.

THE LION IN LOVE

A Lion demanded the daughter of a woodcutter in marriage. The Father, unwilling to grant, and yet afraid to refuse his request, hit upon this expedient to rid himself of his importunities. He expressed his willingness to accept the Lion as the suitor of his daughter on one condition: that he should allow him to extract his teeth, and cut off his claws, as his daughter was fearfully afraid of both. The Lion cheerfully assented to the proposal. But when the toothless, clawless Lion returned to repeat his request, the Woodman, no longer afraid, set upon him with his club, and drove him away into the forest.

THE LABORER AND
THE SNAKE

A Snake, having made his hole close to the porch of a cottage, inflicted a mortal bite on the Cottager's infant son. Grieving over his loss, the Father resolved to kill the Snake. The next day, when it came out of its hole for food, he took up his axe, but by swinging too hastily, missed its head and cut off only the end of its tail. After some time the Cottager, afraid that the Snake would bite him also, endeavored to make peace, and placed some bread and salt in the hole. The Snake, slightly hissing, said: "There can henceforth be no peace between us; for whenever I see you I shall remember the loss of my tail, and whenever you see me you will be thinking of the death of your son."

No one truly forgets injuries in the presence of him who caused the injury.

THE WOLF IN SHEEP'S CLOTHING

Once upon a time a Wolf resolved to disguise his appearance in order to secure food more easily. Encased in the skin of a sheep, he pastured with the flock deceiving the shepherd by his costume. In the evening he was shut up by the shepherd in the fold; the gate was closed, and the entrance made thoroughly secure. But the shepherd, returning to the fold during the night to obtain meat for the next day, mistakenly caught up the Wolf instead of a sheep, and killed him instantly.

Harm seek, harm find.

THE ASS AND THE MULE

A Muleteer set forth on a journey, driving before him an Ass and a Mule, both well laden. The Ass, as long as he traveled along the plain, carried his load with ease, but when he began to ascend the steep path of the mountain, felt his load to be more than he could bear. He entreated his companion to relieve him of a small portion, that he might carry home the rest; but the Mule paid no attention to the request. The Ass shortly afterwards fell down dead under his burden. Not knowing what else to do in so wild a region, the Muleteer placed upon the Mule the load carried by the Ass in addition to his own, and at the top of all placed the hide of the Ass, after he had skinned him. The Mule, groaning beneath his heavy burden, said to himself: "I am treated according to my deserts. If I had only been willing to assist the Ass a little in his need, I should not now be bearing, together with his burden, himself as well."

THE FROGS ASKING FOR A KING

The Frogs, grieved at having no established Ruler, sent ambassadors to Jupiter entreating for a King. Perceiving their simplicity, he cast down a huge log into the lake. The Frogs were terrified at the splash occasioned by its fall and hid themselves in the depths of the pool. But as soon as they realized that the huge log was motionless, they swam again to the top of the water, dismissed their fears, climbed up, and began squatting on it in contempt. After some time they began to think themselves ill-treated in the appointment of so inert a Ruler, and sent a second deputation to Jupiter to pray that he would set over them another sovereign. He then gave them an Eel to govern them. When the Frogs discovered his easy good nature, they sent yet a third time to Jupiter to beg him to choose for them still another King. Jupiter, displeased with all their complaints, sent a Heron, who preyed upon the Frogs day by day till there were none left to croak upon the lake.

THE BOYS AND THE FROGS

Some boys, playing near a pond, saw a number of Frogs in the water and began to pelt them with stones. They killed several of them, when one of the Frogs, lifting his head out of the water, cried out: "Pray stop, my boys: what is sport to you, is death to us."

THE SICK STAG

A sick stag lay down in a quiet corner of its pasture-ground. His companions came in great numbers to inquire after his health, and each one helped himself to a share of the food which had been placed for his use; so that he died, not from his sickness, but from the failure of the means of living.

Evil companions bring more hurt than profit.

THE SALT MERCHANT AND HIS ASS

A Peddler drove his Ass to the seashore to buy salt. His road home lay across a stream into which his Ass, making a false step, fell by accident and rose up again with his load considerably lighter, as the water melted the sack. The Peddler retraced his steps and refilled his panniers with a larger quantity of salt than before. When he came again to the stream, the Ass fell down on purpose in the same spot, and, regaining his feet with the weight of his load much diminished, brayed triumphantly as if he had obtained what he desired. The Peddler saw through his trick and drove him for the third time to the coast, where he bought a cargo of sponges instead of salt. The Ass, again playing the fool, fell down on purpose when he reached the stream, but the sponges became swollen with water, greatly increasing his load. And thus his trick recoiled on him, for he now carried on his back a double burden.

THE OXEN AND
THE BUTCHERS

The Oxen once upon a time sought to destroy the Butchers, who practiced a trade destructive to their race. They assembled on a certain day to carry out their purpose, and sharpened their horns for the contest. But one of them who was exceedingly old (for many a field had he plowed) thus spoke: "These Butchers, it is true, slaughter us, but they do so with skillful hands, and with no unnecessary pain. If we get rid of them, we shall fall into the hands of unskillful operators, and thus suffer a double death: for you may be assured, that though all the Butchers should perish, yet will men never want beef."

Do not be in a hurry to change one evil for another.

THE LION, THE MOUSE, AND THE FOX

A Lion, fatigued by the heat of a summer's day, fell fast asleep in his den. A Mouse ran over his mane and ears and woke him from his slumbers. He rose up and shook himself in great wrath, and searched every corner of his den to find the Mouse. A Fox seeing him said: "A fine Lion you are, to be frightened of a Mouse." "'Tis not the Mouse I fear," said the Lion; "I resent his familiarity and ill-breeding."

Little liberties are great offenses.

THE VAIN JACKDAW

Jupiter determined, it is said, to create a sovereign over the birds, and made proclamation that on a certain day they should all present themselves before him, when he would himself choose the most beautiful among them to be king. The Jackdaw, knowing his own ugliness, searched through the woods and fields, and collected the feathers which had fallen from the wings of his companions, and stuck them in all parts of his body, hoping thereby to make himself the most beautiful of all. When the appointed day arrived, and the birds had assembled before Jupiter, the Jackdaw also made his appearance in his many feathered finery. But when Jupiter proposed to make him king because of the beauty of his plumage, the birds indignantly protested, and each plucked from him his own feathers, leaving the Jackdaw nothing but a Jackdaw.

THE GOATHERD AND
THE WILD GOATS

A Goatherd, driving his flock from their pasture at eventide, found some Wild Goats mingled among them, and shut them up together with his own for the night. The next day it snowed very hard, so that he could not take the herd to their usual feeding places, but was obliged to keep them in the fold. He gave his own goats just sufficient food to keep them alive, but fed the strangers more abundantly in the hope of enticing them to stay with him and of making them his own. When the thaw set in, he led them all out to feed, and the Wild Goats scampered away as fast as they could to the mountains. The Goatherd scolded them for their ingratitude in leaving him, when during the storm he had taken more care of them than of his own herd. One of them, turning about, said to him: "That is the very reason why we are so cautious; for if you yesterday treated us better than the Goats you have had so long, it is plain also that if others came after us, you would in the same manner prefer them to ourselves."

**OLD FRIENDS CANNOT
WITH IMPUNITY BE
SACRIFICED FOR NEW
ONES.**

THE MISCHIEVOUS DOG

A Dog used to run up quietly to the heels of everyone he met, and to bite them without notice. His master suspended a bell about his neck so that the Dog might give notice of his presence wherever he went. Thinking it a mark of distinction, the Dog grew proud of his bell and went tinkling it all over the marketplace. One day an old hound said to him: "Why do you make such an exhibition of yourself? That bell that you carry is not, believe me, any order of merit, but on the contrary a mark of disgrace, a public notice to all men to avoid you as an ill mannered dog."

Notoriety is often mistaken for fame.

THE FOX WHO HAD LOST HIS TAIL

A Fox caught in a trap escaped, but in so doing lost his tail. Thereafter, feeling his life a burden from the shame and ridicule to which he was exposed, he schemed to convince all the other Foxes that being tailless was much more attractive, thus making up for his own deprivation. He assembled a good many Foxes and publicly advised them to cut off their tails, saying that they would not only look much better without them, but that they would get rid of the weight of the brush, which was a very great inconvenience. One of them interrupting him said, "If you had not yourself lost your tail, my friend, you would not thus counsel us."

THE BOY AND THE NETTLES

A Boy was stung by a Nettle. He ran home and told his Mother, saying, "Although it hurts me very much, I only touched it gently." "That was just why it stung you," said his Mother. "The next time you touch a Nettle, grasp it boldly, and it will be soft as silk to your hand, and not in the least hurt you."

Whatever you do, do with all your might.

THE MAN AND HIS TWO SWEETHEARTS

A middle-aged man, whose hair had begun to turn gray, courted two women at the same time. One of them was young, and the other well advanced in years. The elder woman, ashamed to be courted by a man younger than herself, made a point, whenever her admirer visited her, to pull out some portion of his black hairs. The younger, on the contrary, not wishing to become the wife of an old man, was equally zealous in removing every gray hair she could find. Thus it came to pass that between them both he very soon found that he had not a hair left on his head.

Those who seek to please everybody please nobody.

THE ASTRONOMER

An Astronomer used to go out at night to observe the stars. One evening, as he wandered through the suburbs with his whole attention fixed on the sky, he fell accidentally into a deep well. While he lamented and bewailed his sores and bruises, and cried loudly for help, a neighbor ran to the well, and learning what had happened said: "Hark ye, old fellow, why, in striving to pry into what is in heaven, do you not manage to see what is on earth?"

THE WOLVES AND
THE SHEEP

"Why should there always be this fear and slaughter between us?" said the Wolves to the Sheep. "Those evil-disposed Dogs have much to answer for. They always bark whenever we approach you and attack us before we have done any harm. If you would only dismiss them from your heels, there might soon be treaties of peace and reconciliation between us." The Sheep, poor silly creatures, were easily beguiled and dismissed the Dogs, whereupon the Wolves destroyed the unguarded flock at their own pleasure.

THE OLD WOMAN AND
THE PHYSICIAN

An old woman having lost the use of her eyes, called in a Physician to heal them, and made this bargain with him in the presence of witnesses: that if he should cure her blindness, he should receive from her a sum of money; but if her infirmity remained, she should give him nothing. This agreement being made, the Physician, time after time, applied his salve to her eyes, and on every visit took something away, stealing all her property little by little. And when he had got all she had, he healed her and demanded the promised payment. The Old Woman, when she recovered her sight and saw none of her goods in her house, would give him nothing. The Physician insisted on his claim, and, as she still refused, summoned her before the Judge. The Old Woman, standing up in the Court, argued: "This man here speaks the truth in what he says; for I did promise to give him a sum of money if I should recover my sight: but if I continued blind, I was to give him nothing. Now he declares that I am healed. I on the contrary affirm that I am still blind; for when I lost the use of my eyes, I saw in my house various chattels and valuable goods: but now, though he swears I am cured of my blindness, I am not able to see a single thing in it."

THE FIGHTING COCKS
AND THE EAGLE

Two game cocks were fiercely fighting for the mastery of the farmyard. One at last put the other to flight. The vanquished Cock skulked away and hid himself in a quiet corner, while the conqueror, flying up to a high wall, flapped his wings and crowed exultingly with all his might. An Eagle sailing through the air pounced upon him and carried him off in his talons. The vanquished Cock immediately came out of his corner, and ruled henceforth with undisputed mastery.

Pride goes before destruction.

THE CHARGER AND
THE MILLER

A Charger, feeling the infirmities of age, was sent to work in a mill instead of going out to battle. But when he was compelled to grind instead of serving in the wars, he bewailed his change of fortune and called to mind his former state, saying, "Ah! Miller, I had indeed to go campaigning before, but I was barbed from counter to tail, and a man went along to groom me; and now I cannot understand what ailed me to prefer the mill before the battle." "Forbear," said the Miller to him, "harping on what was of yore, for it is the common lot of mortals to sustain the ups and downs of fortune."

THE FOX AND THE MONKEY

A Monkey once danced in an assembly of the Beasts, and so pleased them all by his performance that they elected him their King. A Fox, envying him the honor, discovered a piece of meat lying in a trap, and leading the Monkey to the place where it was, said that she had found a store, but had not used it, she had kept it for him as treasure trove of his kingdom, and counseled him to lay hold of it. The Monkey approached carelessly and was caught in the trap; and on his accusing the Fox of purposely leading him into the snare, she replied, "O Monkey, and are you, with such a mind as yours, going to be King over the Beasts?"

THE HORSE AND HIS RIDER

A Horse Soldier took the utmost pains with his charger. As long as the war lasted, he looked upon him as his fellow-helper in all emergencies and fed him carefully with hay and corn. But when the war was over, he only allowed him chaff to eat and made him carry heavy loads of wood, subjecting him to much slavish drudgery and ill-treatment. War was again proclaimed, however, and when the trumpet summoned him to his standard, the Soldier put on his charger its military trappings, and mounted, being clad in his heavy coat of mail. The Horse fell down straightway under the weight, no longer equal to the burden, and said to his master, "You must now go to the war on foot, for you have transformed me from a Horse into an Ass; and how can you expect that I can again turn in a moment from an Ass to a Horse?"

THE BELLY AND
THE MEMBERS

The members of the Body rebelled against the Belly, and said, "Why should we be perpetually engaged in administering to your wants, while you do nothing but take your rest, and enjoy yourself in luxury and self-indulgence?" The Members carried out their resolve and refused their assistance to the Belly. The whole Body quickly became debilitated, and the hands, feet, mouth, and eyes, when too late, repented of their folly.

THE VINE AND THE GOAT

A Vine was luxuriant in the time of vintage with leaves and grapes. A Goat, passing by, nibbled its young tendrils and its leaves. The Vine addressed him and said: "Why do you thus injure me without a cause, and crop my leaves? Is there no young grass left? But I shall not have to wait long for my just revenge; for if you now should crop my leaves, and cut me down to my root, I shall provide the wine to pour over you when you are led as a victim to the sacrifice."

JUPITER AND THE MONKEY

Jupiter issued a proclamation to all the beasts of the forest and promised a royal reward to the one whose offspring should be deemed the handsomest. The Monkey came with the rest and presented, with all a mother's tenderness, a flat-nosed, hairless, ill-featured young Monkey as a candidate for the promised reward. A general laugh saluted her on the presentation of her son. She resolutely said, "I know not whether Jupiter will allot the prize to my son, but this I do know, that he is at least in the eyes of me his mother, the dearest, handsomest, and most beautiful of all."

THE WIDOW AND
HER LITTLE MAIDENS

A Widow who was fond of cleaning had two little maidens to wait on her. She was in the habit of waking them early in the morning, at cockcrow. The Maidens, aggravated by such excessive labor, resolved to kill the cock who roused their mistress so early. When they had done this, they found that they had only prepared for themselves greater troubles, for their mistress, no longer hearing the hour from the cock, woke them up to their work in the middle of the night.

THE SHEPHERD'S BOY AND THE WOLF

A Shepherd-boy, who watched a flock of sheep near a village, brought out the villagers three or four times by crying out, "Wolf! Wolf!" and when his neighbors came to help him, laughed at them for their pains. The Wolf, however, did truly come at last. The Shepherd-boy, now really alarmed, shouted in an agony of terror: "Pray, do come and help me; the Wolf is killing the sheep;" but no one paid any heed to his cries, nor rendered any assistance. The Wolf, having no cause of fear, at his leisure lacerated or destroyed the whole flock.

There is no believing a liar, even when he speaks the truth.

THE CAT AND THE BIRDS

A Cat, hearing that the Birds in a certain aviary were ailing dressed himself up as a physician, and, taking his cane and a bag of instruments becoming his profession, went to call on them. He knocked at the door and inquired of the inmates how they all did, saying that if they were ill, he would be happy to prescribe for them and cure them. They replied, "We are all very well, and shall continue so, if you will only be good enough to go away, and leave us as we are."

THE KID AND THE WOLF

A Kid standing on the roof of a house, out of harm's way, saw a Wolf passing by and immediately began to taunt and revile him. The Wolf, looking up, said, "Sirrah! I hear thee: yet it is not thou who mockest me, but the roof on which thou art standing."

Time and place often give the advantage to the weak over the strong.

THE OX AND THE FROG

An Ox drinking at a pool trod on a brood of young frogs and crushed one of them to death. The Mother coming up, and missing one of her sons, inquired of his brothers what had become of him. "He is dead, dear Mother; for just now a very huge beast with four great feet came to the pool and crushed him to death with his cloven heel." The Frog, puffing herself out, inquired, "if the beast was as big as that in size." "Cease, Mother, to puff yourself out," said her son, "and do not be angry; for you would, I assure you, sooner burst than successfully imitate the hugeness of that monster."

THE SHEPHERD AND
THE WOLF

A Shepherd once found the whelp of a Wolf and brought it up, and after a while taught it to steal lambs from the neighboring flocks. The Wolf, having shown himself an apt pupil, said to the Shepherd, "Since you have taught me to steal, you must keep a sharp look out, or you will lose some of your own flock."

THE FATHER AND HIS TWO DAUGHTERS

A man had two daughters, the one married to a gardener, and the other to a tile-maker. After a time he went to the daughter who had married the gardener, and inquired how she was and how all things went with her. She said, "All things are prospering with me, and I have only one wish, that there may be a heavy fall of rain, in order that the plants may be well watered." Not long after, he went to the daughter who had married the tilemaker, and likewise inquired of her how she fared; she replied, "I want for nothing, and have only one wish, that the dry weather may continue, and the sun shine hot and bright, so that the bricks might be dried." He said to her, "If your sister wishes for rain, and you for dry weather, with which of the two am I to join my wishes?"

THE FARMER AND HIS SONS

A father, being on the point of death, wished to be sure that his sons would give the same attention to his farm as he himself had given it. He called them to his bedside and said, "My sons, there is a great treasure hid in one of my vineyards." The sons, after his death, took their spades and mattocks and carefully dug over every portion of their land. They found no treasure, but the vines repaid their labor by an extraordinary and superabundant crop.

THE CRAB AND
ITS MOTHER

A Crab said to her son, "Why do you walk so one-sided, my child? It is far more becoming to go straight forward." The young Crab replied: "Quite true, dear Mother; and if you will show me the straight way, I will promise to walk in it." The Mother tried in vain, and submitted without remonstrance to the reproof of her child.

Example is more powerful than precept.

THE HEIFER AND THE OX

A Heifer saw an Ox hard at work harnessed to a plow, and tormented him with reflections on his unhappy fate in being compelled to labor. Shortly afterwards, at the harvest festival, the owner released the Ox from his yoke, but bound the Heifer with cords and led him away to the altar to be slain in honor of the occasion. The Ox saw what was being done, and said with a smile to the Heifer: "For this you were allowed to live in idleness, because you were presently to be sacrificed."

THE SWALLOW,
THE SERPENT, AND
THE COURT OF JUSTICE

A Swallow, returning from abroad and especially fond of dwelling with men, built herself a nest in the wall of a Court of Justice and there hatched seven young birds. A Serpent gliding past the nest from its hole in the wall ate up the young unfledged nestlings. The Swallow, finding her nest empty, lamented greatly and exclaimed: "Woe to me a stranger! that in this place where all others' rights are protected, I alone should suffer wrong."

THE THIEF AND
HIS MOTHER

A Boy stole a lesson-book from one of his schoolfellows and took it home to his Mother. She not only abstained from beating him, but encouraged him. He next time stole a cloak and brought it to her, and she again commended him. The youth, advanced to adulthood, proceeded to steal things of still greater value. At last he was caught in the very act, and having his hands bound behind him, was led away to the place of public execution. His Mother followed in the crowd and violently beat her breast in sorrow, whereupon the young man said, "I wish to say something to my Mother in her ear." She came close to him, and he quickly seized her ear with his teeth and bit it off. The Mother upbraided him as an unnatural child, whereon he replied, "Ah! if you had beaten me when I first stole and brought to you that lesson-book, I should not have come to this, nor have been thus led to a disgraceful death."

THE OLD MAN AND DEATH

An Old Man was employed in cutting wood in the forest, and, in carrying the faggots to the city for sale one day, became very wearied with his long journey. He sat down by the wayside, and throwing down his load, besought "Death" to come. "Death" immediately appeared in answer to his summons and asked for what reason he had called him. The Old Man hurriedly replied, "That, lifting up the load, you may place it again upon my shoulders."

THE FIR-TREE AND
THE BRAMBLE

A Fir-tree said boastingly to the Bramble, "You are useful for nothing at all; while I am everywhere used for roofs and houses." The Bramble answered: "You poor creature, if you would only call to mind the axes and saws which are about to hew you down, you would have reason to wish that you had grown up a Bramble, not a Fir-Tree."

Better poverty without care, than riches with.

THE MOUSE, THE FROG,
AND THE HAWK

A Mouse who always lived on the land, by an unlucky chance formed an intimate acquaintance with a Frog, who lived for the most part in the water. The Frog, one day intent on mischief, bound the foot of the Mouse tightly to his own. Thus joined together, the Frog first of all led his friend the Mouse to the meadow where they were accustomed to find their food. After this, he gradually led him towards the pool in which he lived, until reaching the very brink, he suddenly jumped in, dragging the Mouse with him. The Frog enjoyed the water amazingly, and swam croaking about, as if he had done a good deed. The unhappy Mouse was soon suffocated by the water, and his dead body floated about on the surface, tied to the foot of the Frog. A Hawk observed it, and, pouncing upon it with his talons, carried it aloft. The Frog, being still fastened to the leg of the Mouse, was also carried off a prisoner, and was eaten by the Hawk.

Harm hatch, harm catch.

THE MAN BITTEN BY A DOG

A Man who had been bitten by a Dog went about in quest of someone who might heal him. A friend, meeting him and learning what he wanted, said, "If you would be cured, take a piece of bread, and dip it in the blood from your wound, and go and give it to the Dog that bit you." The Man who had been bitten laughed at this advice and said, "Why? If I should do so, it would be as if I should beg every Dog in the town to bite me."

Benefits bestowed upon the evil-disposed increase their means of injuring you.

THE TWO POTS

A River carried down in its stream two Pots, one made of earthenware and the other of brass. The Earthen Pot said to the Brass Pot, "Pray keep at a distance and do not come near me, for if you touch me ever so slightly, I shall be broken in pieces, and besides, I by no means wish to come near you."

Equals make the best friends.

THE WOLF AND THE SHEEP

A Wolf, sorely wounded and bitten by dogs, lay sick and maimed in his lair. Being in want of food, he called to a Sheep who was passing, and asked him to fetch some water from a stream flowing close beside him. "For," he said, "if you will bring me drink, I will find means to provide myself with meat." "Yes," said the Sheep, "if I should bring you the draught, you would doubtless make me provide the meat also."

Hypocritical speeches are easily seen through.

THE AETHIOP

The Purchaser of a black servant was persuaded that the color of his skin arose from dirt contracted through the neglect of his former masters. On bringing him home he resorted to every means of cleaning, and subjected the man to incessant scrubbings. The servant caught a severe cold, but he never changed his color or complexion.

What's bred in the bone will stick to the flesh.

THE FISHERMAN
AND HIS NETS

A Fisherman, engaged in his calling, made a very successful cast and captured a great haul of fish. He managed by a skillful handling of his net to retain all the large fish and to draw them to the shore; but he could not prevent the smaller fish from falling back through the meshes of the net into the sea.

THE HUNTSMAN AND
THE FISHERMAN

A Huntsman, returning with his dogs from the field, fell in by chance with a Fisherman who was bringing home a basket well laden with fish. The Huntsman wished to have the fish, and their owner experienced an equal longing for the contents of the game-bag. They quickly agreed to exchange the produce of their day's sport. Each was so well pleased with his bargain that they made for some time the same exchange day after day. Finally a neighbor said to them, "If you go on in this way, you will soon destroy by frequent use the pleasure of your exchange, and each will again wish to retain the fruits of his own sport."

Abstain and enjoy.

THE OLD WOMAN AND
THE WINE-JAR

An Old Woman found an empty jar which had lately been full of prime old wine and which still retained the fragrant smell of its former contents. She greedily placed it several times to her nose, and drawing it backwards and forwards said, "O most delicious! How nice must the Wine itself have been, when it leaves behind in the very vessel which contained it so sweet a perfume!"

The memory of a good deed lives.

THE FOX AND THE CROW

A Crow having stolen a bit of meat, perched in a tree and held it in her beak. A Fox, seeing this, longed to possess the meat himself, and by a wily stratagem succeeded. "How handsome is the Crow," he exclaimed, "in the beauty of her shape and in the fairness of her complexion! Oh, if her voice were only equal to her beauty, she would deservedly be considered the Queen of Birds!" This he said deceitfully; but the Crow, anxious to refute the reflection cast upon her voice, set up a loud caw and dropped the flesh. The Fox quickly picked it up, and thus addressed the Crow: "My good Crow, your voice is right enough, but your wit is wanting."

THE TWO DOGS

A man had two dogs: a Hound, trained to assist him in his sports, and a Housedog, taught to watch the house. When he returned home after a good day's sport, he always gave the Housedog a large share of his spoil. The Hound, feeling much aggrieved at this, reproached his companion, saying, "It is very hard to have all this labor, while you, who do not assist in the chase, luxuriate on the fruits of my exertions." The Housedog replied, "Do not blame me, my friend, but find fault with the master, who has not taught me to labor, but to depend for subsistence on the labor of others."

Children are not to be blamed for the faults of their parents.

THE STAG IN THE OX-STALL

A Stag, roundly chased by the hounds and blinded by fear to the danger he was running into, took shelter in a farmyard and hid himself in a shed among the oxen. An Ox gave him this kindly warning: "O unhappy creature! why should you thus, of your own accord, incur destruction and trust yourself in the house of your enemy?" The Stag replied: "Only allow me, friend, to stay where I am, and I will undertake to find some favorable opportunity of effecting my escape." At the approach of the evening the herdsman came to feed his cattle, but did not see the Stag; and even the farm-bailiff with several laborers passed through the shed and failed to notice him. The Stag, congratulating himself on his safety, began to express his sincere thanks to the Oxen who had kindly helped him in the hour of need. One of them again answered him: "We indeed wish you well, but the danger is not over. There is one other yet to pass through the shed, who has as it were a hundred eyes, and until he has come and gone, your life is still in peril." At that moment the master himself entered, and having had to complain that his oxen had not been properly fed, he went up to their racks and cried out: "Why is there such a scarcity of fodder? There is not half enough straw for them to lie on. Those lazy fellows have not even swept the cobwebs away." While he thus examined everything in turn, he spied the tips of the antlers of the Stag peeping out of the straw. Then summoning his laborers, he ordered that the Stag should be seized and killed.

THE HAWK, THE KITE, AND THE PIGEONS

The Pigeons, terrified by the appearance of a Kite, called upon the Hawk to defend them. He at once consented. When they had admitted him into the cote, they found that he made more havoc and slew a larger number of them in one day than the Kite could pounce upon in a whole year.

Avoid a remedy that is worse than the disease.

THE WIDOW AND THE SHEEP

A certain poor Widow had one solitary Sheep. At shearing time, wishing to take his fleece and to avoid expense, she sheared him herself, but used the shears so unskillfully that with the fleece she sheared the flesh. The Sheep, writhing with pain, said, "Why do you hurt me so, Mistress? What weight can my blood add to the wool? If you want my flesh, there is the butcher, who will kill me in an instant; but if you want my fleece and wool, there is the shearer, who will shear and not hurt me."

The least outlay is not always the greatest gain.

THE WILD ASS AND THE LION

A wild Ass and a Lion entered into an alliance so that they might capture the beasts of the forest with greater ease. The Lion agreed to assist the Wild Ass with his strength, while the Wild Ass gave the Lion the benefit of his greater speed. When they had taken as many beasts as their necessities required, the Lion undertook to distribute the prey, and for this purpose divided it into three shares. "I will take the first share," he said, "because I am King: and the second share, as a partner with you in the chase: and the third share (believe me) will be a source of great evil to you, unless you willingly resign it to me, and set off as fast as you can."

Might makes right.

THE EAGLE AND THE ARROW

An Eagle sat on a lofty rock, watching the movements of a Hare whom he sought to make his prey. An archer, who saw the Eagle from a place of concealment, took an accurate aim and wounded him mortally. The Eagle gave one look at the arrow that had entered his heart and saw in that single glance that its feathers had been furnished by himself. "It is a double grief to me," he exclaimed, "that I should perish by an arrow feathered from my own wings."

THE SICK KITE

A Kite, sick unto death, said to his mother: "O Mother! do not mourn, but at once invoke the gods that my life may be prolonged." She replied, "Alas! my son, which of the gods do you think will pity you? Is there one whom you have not outraged by filching from their very altars a part of the sacrifice offered up to them?"

We must make friends in prosperity if we would have their help in adversity.

THE LION AND THE DOLPHIN

A Lion roaming by the seashore saw a Dolphin lift up its head out of the waves, and suggested that they contract an alliance, saying that of all the animals they ought to be the best friends, since the one was the king of beasts on the earth, and the other was the sovereign ruler of all the inhabitants of the ocean. The Dolphin gladly consented to this request. Not long afterwards the Lion had a combat with a wild bull, and called on the Dolphin to help him. The Dolphin, though quite willing to give him assistance, was unable to do so, as he could not by any means reach the land. The Lion abused him as a traitor. The Dolphin replied, "Nay, my friend, blame not me, but Nature, which, while giving me the sovereignty of the sea, has quite denied me the power of living upon the land."

THE LION AND THE BOAR

On a summer day, when the great heat induced a general thirst among the beasts, a Lion and a Boar came at the same moment to a small well to drink. They fiercely disputed which of them should drink first, and were soon engaged in the agonies of a mortal combat. When they stopped suddenly to catch their breath for a fiercer renewal of the fight, they saw some Vultures waiting in the distance to feast on the one that should fall first. They at once made up their quarrel, saying, "It is better for us to make friends, than to become the food of Crows or Vultures."

THE ONE-EYED DOE

A Doe blind in one eye was accustomed to graze as near to the edge of the cliff as she possibly could, in the hope of securing her greater safety. She turned her sound eye towards the land that she might get the earliest tidings of the approach of hunter or hound, and her injured eye towards the sea, from whence she entertained no anticipation of danger. Some boatmen sailing by saw her, and taking a successful aim, mortally wounded her. Yielding up her last breath, she gasped forth this lament: "O wretched creature that I am! to take such precaution against the land, and after all to find this seashore, to which I had come for safety, so much more perilous."

THE SHEPHERD AND
THE SEA

A Shepherd, keeping watch over his sheep near the shore, saw the Sea very calm and smooth, and longed to make a voyage with a view to commerce. He sold all his flock, invested it in a cargo of dates, and set sail. But a very great tempest came on, and the ship being in danger of sinking, he threw all his merchandise overboard, and barely escaped with his life in the empty ship. Not long afterwards when someone passed by and observed the unruffled calm of the Sea, he interrupted him and said, "It is again in want of dates, and therefore looks quiet."

THE ASS, THE COCK, AND THE LION

An Ass and a Cock were in a straw-yard together when a Lion, desperate from hunger, approached the spot. He was about to spring upon the Ass, when the Cock (to the sound of whose voice the Lion, it is said, has a singular aversion) crowed loudly, and the Lion fled away as fast as he could. The Ass, observing his trepidation at the mere crowing of a Cock summoned courage to attack him, and galloped after him for that purpose. He had run no long distance, when the Lion, turning about, seized him and tore him to pieces.

False confidence often leads into danger.

THE MICE AND
THE WEASELS

The Weasels and the Mice waged a perpetual war with each other, in which much blood was shed. The Weasels were always the victors. The Mice thought that the cause of their frequent defeats was that they had no leaders set apart from the general army to command them, and that they were exposed to dangers from lack of discipline. They therefore chose as leaders Mice that were most renowned for their family descent, strength, and counsel, as well as those most noted for their courage in the fight, so that they might be better marshaled in battle array and formed into troops, regiments, and battalions. When all this was done, and the army disciplined, and the herald Mouse had duly proclaimed war by challenging the Weasels, the newly chosen generals bound their heads with straws, that they might be more conspicuous to all their troops. Scarcely had the battle begun, when a great rout overwhelmed the Mice, who scampered off as fast as they could to their holes. The generals, not being able to get in on account of the ornaments on their heads, were all captured and eaten by the Weasels.

The more honor the more danger.

THE MICE IN COUNCIL

The Mice summoned a council to decide how they might best devise means of warning themselves of the approach of their great enemy the Cat. Among the many plans suggested, the one that found most favor was the proposal to tie a bell to the neck of the Cat, so that the Mice, being warned by the sound of the tinkling, might run away and hide themselves in their holes at his approach. But when the Mice further debated who among them should thus "bell the Cat", there was no one found to do it.

THE WOLF AND
THE HOUSEDOG

A Wolf, meeting a big well-fed Mastiff with a wooden collar about his neck asked him who it was that fed him so well and yet compelled him to drag that heavy log about wherever he went. "The master," he replied. Then said the Wolf: "May no friend of mine ever be in such a plight; for the weight of this chain is enough to spoil the appetite."

THE RIVERS AND THE SEA

The Rivers joined together to complain to the Sea, saying, "Why is it that when we flow into your tides so potable and sweet, you work in us such a change, and make us salty and unfit to drink?" The Sea, perceiving that they intended to throw the blame on him, said, "Pray cease to flow into me, and then you will not be made briny."

THE PLAYFUL ASS

An Ass climbed up to the roof of a building, and frisking about there, broke in the tiling. The owner went up after him and quickly drove him down, beating him severely with a thick wooden cudgel. The Ass said, "Why, I saw the Monkey do this very thing yesterday, and you all laughed heartily, as if it afforded you very great amusement."

THE THREE TRADESMEN

A great city was besieged, and its inhabitants were called together to consider the best means of protecting it from the enemy. A Bricklayer earnestly recommended bricks as affording the best material for an effective resistance. A Carpenter, with equal enthusiasm, proposed timber as a preferable method of defense. Upon which a Currier stood up and said, "Sirs, I differ from you altogether: there is no material for resistance equal to a covering of hides; and nothing so good as leather."

Every man for himself.

THE MASTER AND
HIS DOGS

A certain Man, detained by a storm in his country house, first of all killed his sheep, and then his goats, for the maintenance of his household. The storm still continuing, he was obliged to slaughter his yoke oxen for food. On seeing this, his Dogs took counsel together, and said, "It is time for us to be off, for if the master spare not his oxen, who work for his gain, how can we expect him to spare us?"

He is not to be trusted as a friend who mistreats his own family.

THE WOLF AND
THE SHEPHERDS

A Wolf, passing by, saw some Shepherds in a hut eating a haunch of mutton for their dinner. Approaching them, he said, "What a clamor you would raise if I were to do as you are doing!"

THE DOLPHINS,
THE WHALES, AND
THE SPRAT

The Dolphins and Whales waged a fierce war with each other. When the battle was at its height, a Sprat lifted its head out of the waves and said that he would reconcile their differences if they would accept him as an umpire. One of the Dolphins replied, "We would far rather be destroyed in our battle with each other than admit any interference from you in our affairs."

THE ASS CARRYING
THE IMAGE

An Ass once carried through the streets of a city a famous wooden Image, to be placed in one of its Temples. As he passed along, the crowd made lowly prostration before the Image. The Ass, thinking that they bowed their heads in token of respect for himself, bristled up with pride, gave himself airs, and refused to move another step. The Driver, seeing him thus stop, laid his whip lustily about his shoulders and said, "O you perverse dull-head! it is not yet come to this, that men pay worship to an Ass."

They are not wise who give to themselves the credit due to others.

THE TWO TRAVELERS AND THE AXE

Two Men were journeying together. One of them picked up an axe that lay upon the path, and said, "I have found an axe." "Nay, my friend," replied the other, "do not say 'I', but 'We' have found an axe." They had not gone far before they saw the owner of the axe pursuing them, and he who had picked up the axe said, "We are undone." "Nay," replied the other, "keep to your first mode of speech, my friend; what you thought right then, think right now. Say 'I', not 'We' are undone."

He who shares the danger ought to share the prize.

THE OLD LION

A Lion, worn out with years and powerless from disease, lay on the ground at the point of death. A Boar rushed upon him, and avenged with a stroke of his tusks a long-remembered injury. Shortly afterwards the Bull with his horns gored him as if he were an enemy. When the Ass saw that the huge beast could be assailed with impunity, he let drive at his forehead with his heels. The expiring Lion said, "I have reluctantly brooked the insults of the brave, but to be compelled to endure such treatment from thee, a disgrace to Nature, is indeed to die a double death."

THE OLD HOUND

A Hound, who in the days of his youth and strength had never yielded to any beast of the forest, encountered in his old age a boar in the chase. He seized him boldly by the ear, but could not retain his hold because of the decay of his teeth, so that the boar escaped. His master, quickly coming up, was very much disappointed, and fiercely abused the dog. The Hound looked up and said, "It was not my fault master: my spirit was as good as ever, but I could not help my infirmities. I rather deserve to be praised for what I have been, than to be blamed for what I am."

THE BEE AND JUPITER

A Bee from Mount Hymettus, the queen of the hive, ascended to Olympus to present Jupiter some honey fresh from her combs. Jupiter, delighted with the offering of honey, promised to give whatever she should ask. She therefore besought him, saying, "Give me, I pray thee, a sting, that if any mortal shall approach to take my honey, I may kill him." Jupiter was much displeased, for he loved the race of man, but could not refuse the request because of his promise. He thus answered the Bee: "You shall have your request, but it will be at the peril of your own life. For if you use your sting, it shall remain in the wound you make, and then you will die from the loss of it."

Evil wishes, like chickens, come home to roost.

THE MILK-WOMAN AND
HER PAIL

A farmer's daughter was carrying her pail of milk from the field to the farmhouse, when she fell a-musing. "The money for which this milk will be sold, will buy at least three hundred eggs. The eggs, allowing for all mishaps, will produce two hundred and fifty chickens. The chickens will become ready for the market when poultry will fetch the highest price, so that by the end of the year I shall have money enough from my share to buy a new gown. In this dress I will go to the Christmas parties, where all the young fellows will propose to me, but I will toss my head and refuse them every one." At this moment she tossed her head in unison with her thoughts, when down fell the milk pail to the ground, and all her imaginary schemes perished in a moment.

THE SEASIDE TRAVELERS

Some Travelers, journeying along the seashore, climbed to the summit of a tall cliff, and looking over the sea, saw in the distance what they thought was a large ship. They waited in the hope of seeing it enter the harbor, but as the object on which they looked was driven nearer to shore by the wind, they found that it could at the most be a small boat, and not a ship. When however it reached the beach, they discovered that it was only a large faggot of sticks, and one of them said to his companions, "We have waited for no purpose, for after all there is nothing to see but a load of wood."

Our mere anticipations of life outrun its realities.

THE BRAZIER AND HIS DOG

A Brazier had a little Dog, which was a great favorite with his master, and his constant companion. While he hammered away at his metals the Dog slept; but when, on the other hand, he went to dinner and began to eat, the Dog woke up and wagged his tail, as if he would ask for a share of his meal. His master one day, pretending to be angry and shaking his stick at him, said, "You wretched little sluggard! what shall I do to you? While I am hammering on the anvil, you sleep on the mat; and when I begin to eat after my toil, you wake up and wag your tail for food. Do you not know that labor is the source of every blessing, and that none but those who work are entitled to eat?"

THE ASS AND HIS SHADOW

A Traveler hired an Ass to convey him to a distant place. The day being intensely hot, and the sun shining in its strength, the Traveler stopped to rest, and sought shelter from the heat under the Shadow of the Ass. As this afforded only protection for one, and as the Traveler and the owner of the Ass both claimed it, a violent dispute arose between them as to which of them had the right to the Shadow. The owner maintained that he had let the Ass only, and not his Shadow. The Traveler asserted that he had, with the hire of the Ass, hired his Shadow also. The quarrel proceeded from words to blows, and while the men fought, the Ass galloped off.

In quarreling about the shadow we often lose the substance.

THE ASS AND HIS MASTERS

An Ass, belonging to an herb-seller who gave him too little food and too much work made a petition to Jupiter to be released from his present service and provided with another master. Jupiter, after warning him that he would repent his request, caused him to be sold to a tile-maker. Shortly afterwards, finding that he had heavier loads to carry and harder work in the brick-field, he petitioned for another change of master. Jupiter, telling him that it would be the last time that he could grant his request, ordained that he be sold to a tanner. The Ass found that he had fallen into worse hands, and noting his master's occupation, said, groaning: "It would have been better for me to have been either starved by the one, or to have been overworked by the other of my former masters, than to have been bought by my present owner, who will even after I am dead tan my hide, and make me useful to him."

THE OAK AND THE REEDS

A very large Oak was uprooted by the wind and thrown across a stream. It fell among some Reeds, which it thus addressed: "I wonder how you, who are so light and weak, are not entirely crushed by these strong winds." They replied, "You fight and contend with the wind, and consequently you are destroyed; while we on the contrary bend before the least breath of air, and therefore remain unbroken, and escape."

Stoop to conquer.

THE FISHERMAN AND
THE LITTLE FISH

A Fisherman who lived on the produce of his nets, one day caught a single small Fish as the result of his day's labor. The Fish, panting convulsively, thus entreated for his life: "O Sir, what good can I be to you, and how little am I worth? I am not yet come to my full size. Pray spare my life, and put me back into the sea. I shall soon become a large fish fit for the tables of the rich, and then you can catch me again, and make a handsome profit of me." The Fisherman replied, "I should indeed be a very simple fellow if, for the chance of a greater uncertain profit, I were to forego my present certain gain."

THE HUNTER AND
THE WOODMAN

A Hunter, not very bold, was searching for the tracks of a Lion. He asked a man felling oaks in the forest if he had seen any marks of his footsteps or knew where his lair was. "I will," said the man, "at once show you the Lion himself." The Hunter, turning very pale and chattering with his teeth from fear, replied, "No, thank you. I did not ask that; it is his track only I am in search of, not the Lion himself."

The hero is brave in deeds as well as words.

THE WILD BOAR AND
THE FOX

A wild Boar stood under a tree and rubbed his tusks against the trunk. A Fox passing by asked him why he thus sharpened his teeth when there was no danger threatening from either huntsman or hound. He replied, "I do it advisedly; for it would never do to have to sharpen my weapons just at the time I ought to be using them."

THE LION IN A FARMYARD

A Lion entered a farmyard. The Farmer, wishing to catch him, shut the gate. When the Lion found that he could not escape, he flew upon the sheep and killed them, and then attacked the oxen. The Farmer, beginning to be alarmed for his own safety, opened the gate and released the Lion. On his departure the Farmer grievously lamented the destruction of his sheep and oxen, but his wife, who had been a spectator to all that took place, said, "On my word, you are rightly served, for how could you for a moment think of shutting up a Lion along with you in your farmyard when you know that you shake in your shoes if you only hear his roar at a distance?"

MERCURY AND
THE SCULPTOR

Mercury once determined to learn in what esteem he was held among mortals. For this purpose he assumed the character of a man and visited in this disguise a Sculptor's studio having looked at various statues, he demanded the price of two figures of Jupiter and Juno. When the sum at which they were valued was named, he pointed to a figure of himself, saying to the Sculptor, "You will certainly want much more for this, as it is the statue of the Messenger of the Gods, and author of all your gain." The Sculptor replied, "Well, if you will buy these, I'll fling you that into the bargain."

THE SWAN AND THE GOOSE

A certain rich man bought in the market a Goose and a Swan. He fed the one for his table and kept the other for the sake of its song. When the time came for killing the Goose, the cook went to get him at night, when it was dark, and he was not able to distinguish one bird from the other. By mistake he caught the Swan instead of the Goose. The Swan, threatened with death, burst forth into song and thus made himself known by his voice, and preserved his life by his melody.

THE SWOLLEN FOX

A very hungry Fox, seeing some bread and meat left by shepherds in the hollow of an oak, crept into the hole and made a hearty meal. When he finished, he was so full that he was not able to get out, and began to groan and lament his fate. Another Fox passing by heard his cries, and coming up, inquired the cause of his complaining. On learning what had happened, he said to him, "Ah, you will have to remain there, my friend, until you become such as you were when you crept in, and then you will easily get out."

THE FOX AND
THE WOODCUTTER

A Fox, running before the hounds, came across a Woodcutter felling an oak and begged him to show him a safe hiding-place. The Woodcutter advised him to take shelter in his own hut, so the Fox crept in and hid himself in a corner. The huntsman soon came up with his hounds and inquired of the Woodcutter if he had seen the Fox. He declared that he had not seen him, and yet pointed, all the time he was speaking, to the hut where the Fox lay hidden. The huntsman took no notice of the signs, but believing his word, hastened forward in the chase. As soon as they were well away, the Fox departed without taking any notice of the Woodcutter: whereon he called to him and reproached him, saying, "You ungrateful fellow, you owe your life to me, and yet you leave me without a word of thanks." The Fox replied, "Indeed, I should have thanked you fervently if your deeds had been as good as your words, and if your hands had not been traitors to your speech."

THE BIRDCATCHER,
THE PARTRIDGE, AND
THE COCK

A Birdcatcher was about to sit down to a dinner of herbs when a friend unexpectedly came in. The bird-trap was quite empty, as he had caught nothing, and he had to kill a pied Partridge, which he had tamed for a decoy. The bird entreated earnestly for his life: "What would you do without me when next you spread your nets? Who would chirp you to sleep, or call for you the covey of answering birds?" The Birdcatcher spared his life, and determined to pick out a fine young Cock just attaining to his comb. But the Cock expostulated in piteous tones from his perch: "If you kill me, who will announce to you the appearance of the dawn? Who will wake you to your daily tasks or tell you when it is time to visit the bird-trap in the morning?" He replied, "What you say is true. You are a capital bird at telling the time of day. But my friend and I must have our dinners."

Necessity knows no law.

THE MONKEY AND
THE FISHERMEN

A Monkey perched upon a lofty tree saw some Fishermen casting their nets into a river, and narrowly watched their proceedings. The Fishermen after a while gave up fishing, and on going home to dinner left their nets upon the bank. The Monkey, who is the most imitative of animals, descended from the treetop and endeavored to do as they had done. Having handled the net, he threw it into the river, but became tangled in the meshes and drowned. With his last breath he said to himself, "I am rightly served; for what business had I who had never handled a net to try and catch fish?"

THE FLEA AND
THE WRESTLER

A Flea settled upon the bare foot of a Wrestler and bit him, causing the man to call loudly upon Hercules for help. When the Flea a second time hopped upon his foot, he groaned and said, "O Hercules! if you will not help me against a Flea, how can I hope for your assistance against greater antagonists?"

THE TWO FROGS

Two Frogs dwelt in the same pool. When the pool dried up under the summer's heat, they left it and set out together for another home. As they went along they chanced to pass a deep well, amply supplied with water, and when they saw it, one of the Frogs said to the other, "Let us descend and make our abode in this well: it will furnish us with shelter and food." The other replied with greater caution, "But suppose the water should fail us. How can we get out again from so great a depth?"

Do nothing without a regard to the consequences.

THE CAT AND THE MICE

A certain house was overrun with Mice. A Cat, discovering this, made her way into it and began to catch and eat them one by one. Fearing for their lives, the Mice kept themselves close in their holes. The Cat was no longer able to get at them and perceived that she must tempt them forth by some device. For this purpose she jumped upon a peg, and suspending herself from it, pretended to be dead. One of the Mice, peeping stealthily out, saw her and said, "Ah, my good madam, even though you should turn into a meal-bag, we will not come near you."

THE LION, THE BEAR, AND THE FOX

A Lion and a Bear seized a Kid at the same moment, and fought fiercely for its possession. When they had fearfully lacerated each other and were faint from the long combat, they lay down exhausted with fatigue. A Fox, who had gone round them at a distance several times, saw them both stretched on the ground with the Kid lying untouched in the middle. He ran in between them, and seizing the Kid scampered off as fast as he could. The Lion and the Bear saw him, but not being able to get up, said, "Woe be to us, that we should have fought and belabored ourselves only to serve the turn of a Fox."

It sometimes happens that one man has all the toil, and another all the profit.

THE DOE AND THE LION

A Doe hard pressed by hunters sought refuge in a cave belonging to a Lion. The Lion concealed himself on seeing her approach, but when she was safe within the cave, sprang upon her and tore her to pieces. "Woe is me," exclaimed the Doe, "who have escaped from man, only to throw myself into the mouth of a wild beast?"

In avoiding one evil, care must be taken not to fall into another.

THE FARMER AND THE FOX

A Farmer, who bore a grudge against a Fox for robbing his poultry yard, caught him at last, and being determined to take an ample revenge, tied some rope well soaked in oil to his tail, and set it on fire. The Fox by a strange fatality rushed to the fields of the Farmer who had captured him. It was the time of the wheat harvest; but the Farmer reaped nothing that year and returned home grieving sorely.

THE SEAGULL AND
THE KITE

A Seagull having bolted down too large a fish, burst its deep gullet-bag and lay down on the shore to die. A Kite saw him and exclaimed: "You richly deserve your fate; for a bird of the air has no business to seek its food from the sea."

Every man should be content to mind his own business.

THE PHILOSOPHER,
THE ANTS, AND MERCURY

A Philosopher witnessed from the shore the shipwreck of a vessel, of which the crew and passengers were all drowned. He inveighed against the injustice of Providence, which would for the sake of one criminal perchance sailing in the ship allow so many innocent persons to perish. As he was indulging in these reflections, he found himself surrounded by a whole army of Ants, near whose nest he was standing. One of them climbed up and stung him, and he immediately trampled them all to death with his foot. Mercury presented himself, and striking the Philosopher with his wand, said, "And are you indeed to make yourself a judge of the dealings of Providence, who hast thyself in a similar manner treated these poor Ants?"

THE MOUSE AND THE BULL

A Bull was bitten by a Mouse and, angered by the wound, tried to capture him. But the Mouse reached his hole in safety. Though the Bull dug into the walls with his horns, he tired before he could rout out the Mouse, and crouching down, went to sleep outside the hole. The Mouse peeped out, crept furtively up his flank, and again biting him, retreated to his hole. The Bull rising up, and not knowing what to do, was sadly perplexed. At which the Mouse said, "The great do not always prevail. There are times when the small and lowly are the strongest to do mischief."

THE LION AND THE HARE

A Lion came across a Hare, who was fast asleep. He was just in the act of seizing her, when a fine young Hart trotted by, and he left the Hare to follow him. The Hare, scared by the noise, awoke and scudded away. The Lion was unable after a long chase to catch the Hart, and returned to feed upon the Hare. On finding that the Hare also had run off, he said, "I am rightly served, for having let go of the food that I had in my hand for the chance of obtaining more."

THE PEASANT AND
THE EAGLE

A Peasant found an Eagle captured in a trap, and much admiring the bird, set him free. The Eagle did not prove ungrateful to his deliverer, for seeing the Peasant sitting under a wall which was not safe, he flew toward him and with his talons snatched a bundle from his head. When the Peasant rose in pursuit, the Eagle let the bundle fall again. Taking it up, the man returned to the same place, to find that the wall under which he had been sitting had fallen to pieces; and he marveled at the service rendered him by the Eagle.

THE IMAGE OF MERCURY
AND THE CARPENTER

A very poor man, a Carpenter by trade, had a wooden image of Mercury, before which he made offerings day by day, and begged the idol to make him rich, but in spite of his entreaties he became poorer and poorer. At last, being very angry, he took his image down from its pedestal and dashed it against the wall. When its head was knocked off, out came a stream of gold, which the Carpenter quickly picked up and said, "Well, I think thou art altogether contradictory and unreasonable; for when I paid you honor, I reaped no benefits: but now that I maltreat you I am loaded with an abundance of riches."

THE BULL AND THE GOAT

A Bull, escaping from a Lion, hid in a cave which some shepherds had recently occupied. As soon as he entered, a He-Goat left in the cave sharply attacked him with his horns. The Bull quietly addressed him: "Butt away as much as you will. I have no fear of you, but of the Lion. Let that monster go away and I will soon let you know what is the respective strength of a Goat and a Bull."

It shows an evil disposition to take advantage of a friend in distress.

THE DANCING MONKEYS

A Prince had some Monkeys trained to dance. Being naturally great mimics of men's actions, they showed themselves most apt pupils, and when arrayed in their rich clothes and masks, they danced as well as any of the courtiers. The spectacle was often repeated with great applause, till on one occasion a courtier, bent on mischief, took from his pocket a handful of nuts and threw them upon the stage. The Monkeys at the sight of the nuts forgot their dancing and became (as indeed they were) Monkeys instead of actors. Pulling off their masks and tearing their robes, they fought with one another for the nuts. The dancing spectacle thus came to an end amidst the laughter and ridicule of the audience.

THE FOX AND THE LEOPARD

The Fox and the Leopard disputed which was the more beautiful of the two. The Leopard exhibited one by one the various spots which decorated his skin. But the Fox, interrupting him, said, "And how much more beautiful than you am I, who am decorated, not in body, but in mind."

THE MONKEYS AND
THEIR MOTHER

The Monkey, it is said, has two young ones at each birth. The Mother fondles one and nurtures it with the greatest affection and care, but hates and neglects the other. It happened once that the young one which was caressed and loved was smothered by the too great affection of the Mother, while the despised one was nurtured and reared in spite of the neglect to which it was exposed.

The best intentions will not always ensure success.

THE OAKS AND JUPITER

The Oaks presented a complaint to Jupiter, saying, "We bear for no purpose the burden of life, as of all the trees that grow we are the most continually in peril of the axe." Jupiter made answer: "You have only to thank yourselves for the misfortunes to which you are exposed: for if you did not make such excellent pillars and posts, and prove yourselves so serviceable to the carpenters and the farmers, the axe would not so frequently be laid to your roots."

THE HARE AND
THE HOUND

A Hound started a Hare from his lair, but after a long run, gave up the chase. A goat-herd seeing him stop, mocked him, saying "The little one is the best runner of the two." The Hound replied, "You do not see the difference between us: I was only running for a dinner, but he for his life."

THE TRAVELER AND FORTUNE

A Traveler wearied from a long journey lay down, overcome with fatigue, on the very brink of a deep well. Just as he was about to fall into the water, Dame Fortune, it is said, appeared to him and waking him from his slumber thus addressed him: "Good Sir, pray wake up: for if you fall into the well, the blame will be thrown on me, and I shall get an ill name among mortals; for I find that men are sure to impute their calamities to me, however much by their own folly they have really brought them on themselves."

Everyone is more or less master of his own fate.

THE BALD KNIGHT

A bald Knight, who wore a wig, went out to hunt. A sudden puff of wind blew off his hat and wig, at which a loud laugh rang forth from his companions. He pulled up his horse, and with great glee joined in the joke by saying, "What a marvel it is that hairs which are not mine should fly from me, when they have forsaken even the man on whose head they grew."

THE SHEPHERD AND
THE DOG

A Shepherd penning his sheep in the fold for the night was about to shut up a wolf with them, when his Dog perceiving the wolf said, "Master, how can you expect the sheep to be safe if you admit a wolf into the fold?"

THE LAMP

A Lamp, soaked with too much oil and flaring brightly, boasted that it gave more light than the sun. Then a sudden puff of wind arose, and the Lamp was immediately extinguished. Its owner lit it again, and said: "Boast no more, but henceforth be content to give thy light in silence. Know that not even the stars need to be relit."

THE LION, THE FOX, AND THE ASS

The Lion, the Fox and the Ass entered into an agreement to assist each other in the chase. Having secured a large booty, the Lion on their return from the forest asked the Ass to allot his due portion to each of the three partners in the treaty. The Ass carefully divided the spoil into three equal shares and modestly requested the two others to make the first choice. The Lion, bursting out into a great rage, devoured the Ass. Then he requested the Fox to do him the favor to make a division. The Fox accumulated all that they had killed into one large heap and left to himself the smallest possible morsel. The Lion said, "Who has taught you, my very excellent fellow, the art of division? You are perfect to a fraction." He replied, "I learned it from the Ass, by witnessing his fate."

Happy is the man who learns from the misfortunes of others.

THE BULL, THE LIONESS, AND THE WILD-BOAR HUNTER

A Bull finding a lion's cub asleep gored him to death with his horns. The Lioness came up, and bitterly lamented the death of her whelp. A wild-boar Hunter, seeing her distress, stood at a distance and said to her, "Think how many men there are who have reason to lament the loss of their children, whose deaths have been caused by you."

THE OAK AND
THE WOODCUTTERS

The Woodcutter cut down a Mountain Oak and split it in pieces, making wedges of its own branches for dividing the trunk. The Oak said with a sigh, "I do not care about the blows of the axe aimed at my roots, but I do grieve at being torn in pieces by these wedges made from my own branches."

Misfortunes springing from ourselves are the hardest to bear.

THE HEN AND
THE GOLDEN EGGS

A Cottager and his wife had a Hen that laid a golden egg every day. They supposed that the Hen must contain a great lump of gold in its inside, and in order to get the gold they killed it. Having done so, they found to their surprise that the Hen differed in no respect from their other hens. The foolish pair, thus hoping to become rich all at once, deprived themselves of the gain of which they were assured day by day.

THE ASS AND THE FROGS

An Ass, carrying a load of wood, passed through a pond. As he was crossing through the water he lost his footing, stumbled and fell, and not being able to rise on account of his load, groaned heavily. Some Frogs frequenting the pool heard his lamentation, and said, "What would you do if you had to live here always as we do, when you make such a fuss about a mere fall into the water?"

MEN OFTEN BEAR LITTLE GRIEVANCES WITH LESS COURAGE THAN THEY DO LARGE MISFORTUNES.

THE CROW AND THE RAVEN

A Crow was jealous of the Raven, because he was considered a bird of good omen and always attracted the attention of men, who noted by his flight the good or evil course of future events. Seeing some travelers approaching, the Crow flew up into a tree, and perching herself on one of the branches, cawed as loudly as she could. The travelers turned towards the sound and wondered what it foreboded, when one of them said to his companion, "Let us proceed on our journey, my friend, for it is only the caw of a crow, and her cry, you know, is no omen."

Those who assume a character which does not belong to them, only make themselves ridiculous.

THE TREES AND THE AXE

A Man came into a forest and asked the Trees to provide him a handle for his axe. The Trees consented to his request and gave him a young ash-tree. No sooner had the Man fitted a new handle to his axe from it, than he began to use it and quickly felled with his strokes the noblest giants of the forest. An old oak, lamenting when too late the destruction of his companions, said to a neighboring cedar, "The first step has lost us all. If we had not given up the rights of the ash, we might yet have retained our own privileges and have stood for ages."

THE CRAB AND THE FOX

A Crab, forsaking the seashore, chose a neighboring green meadow as its feeding ground. A Fox came across him, and being very hungry ate him up. Just as he was on the point of being eaten, the Crab said, "I well deserve my fate, for what business had I on the land, when by my nature and habits I am only adapted for the sea?"

Contentment with our lot is an element of happiness.

THE WOMAN AND HER HEN

A Woman possessed a Hen that gave her an egg every day. She often pondered how she might obtain two eggs daily instead of one, and at last, to gain her purpose, determined to give the Hen a double allowance of barley. From that day the Hen became fat and sleek, and never once laid another egg.

THE ASS AND
THE OLD SHEPHERD

A Shepherd, watching his Ass feeding in a meadow, was alarmed all of a sudden by the cries of the enemy. He appealed to the Ass to fly with him, lest they should both be captured, but the animal lazily replied, "Why should I, pray? Do you think it likely the conqueror will place on me two sets of panniers?" "No," rejoined the Shepherd. "Then," said the Ass, "as long as I carry the panniers, what matters it to me whom I serve?"

In a change of government the poor change nothing beyond the name of their master.

THE KITES AND THE SWANS

The Kites of olden times, as well as the Swans, had the privilege of song. But having heard the neigh of the horse, they were so enchanted with the sound, that they tried to imitate it; and, in trying to neigh, they forgot how to sing.

The desire for imaginary benefits often involves the loss of present blessings.

THE WOLVES AND
THE SHEEPDOGS

The Wolves thus addressed the Sheepdogs: "Why should you, who are like us in so many things, not be entirely of one mind with us, and live with us as brothers should? We differ from you in one point only. We live in freedom, but you bow down to and slave for men, who in return for your services flog you with whips and put collars on your necks. They make you also guard their sheep, and while they eat the mutton throw only the bones to you. If you will be persuaded by us, you will give us the sheep, and we will enjoy them in common, till we all are surfeited." The Dogs listened favorably to these proposals, and, entering the den of the Wolves, they were set upon and torn to pieces.

THE HARES AND THE FOXES

The Hares waged war with the Eagles, and called upon the Foxes to help them. They replied, "We would willingly have helped you, if we had not known who you were, and with whom you were fighting."

Count the cost before you commit yourselves.

THE BOWMAN AND LION

A very skillful Bowman went to the mountains in search of game, but all the beasts of the forest fled at his approach. The Lion alone challenged him to combat. The Bowman immediately shot out an arrow and said to the Lion: "I send thee my messenger, that from him thou mayest learn what I myself shall be when I assail thee." The wounded Lion rushed away in great fear, and when a Fox who had seen it all happen told him to be of good courage and not to back off at the first attack he replied: "You counsel me in vain; for if he sends so fearful a messenger, how shall I abide the attack of the man himself?"

Be on guard against men who can strike from a distance.

THE CAMEL

When Man first saw the Camel, he was so frightened at his vast size that he ran away. After a time, perceiving the meekness and gentleness of the beast's temper, he summoned courage enough to approach him. Soon afterwards, observing that he was an animal altogether deficient in spirit, he assumed such boldness as to put a bridle in his mouth, and to let a child drive him.

Use serves to overcome dread.

THE WASP AND THE SNAKE

A Wasp seated himself upon the head of a Snake and, striking him unceasingly with his stings, wounded him to death. The Snake, being in great torment and not knowing how to rid himself of his enemy, saw a wagon heavily laden with wood, and went and purposely placed his head under the wheels, saying, "At least my enemy and I shall perish together."

THE DOG AND THE HARE

A Hound having started a Hare on the hillside pursued her for some distance, at one time biting her with his teeth as if he would take her life, and at another fawning upon her, as if in play with another dog. The Hare said to him, "I wish you would act sincerely by me, and show yourself in your true colors. If you are a friend, why do you bite me so hard? If an enemy, why do you fawn on me?"

No one can be a friend if you know not whether to trust or distrust him.

THE BULL AND THE CALF

A Bull was striving with all his might to squeeze himself through a narrow passage which led to his stall. A young Calf came up, and offered to go before and show him the way by which he could manage to pass. "Save yourself the trouble," said the Bull; "I knew that way long before you were born."

THE STAG, THE WOLF,
AND THE SHEEP

A Stag asked a Sheep to lend him a measure of wheat, and said that the Wolf would be his surety. The Sheep, fearing some fraud was intended, excused herself, saying, "The Wolf is accustomed to seize what he wants and to run off; and you, too, can quickly outstrip me in your rapid flight. How then shall I be able to find you, when the day of payment comes?"

Two blacks do not make one white.

THE PEACOCK AND
THE CRANE

A Peacock spreading its gorgeous tail mocked a Crane that passed by, ridiculing the ashen hue of its plumage and saying, "I am robed, like a king, in gold and purple and all the colors of the rainbow; while you have not a bit of color on your wings." "True," replied the Crane; "but I soar to the heights of heaven and lift up my voice to the stars, while you walk below, like a cock, among the birds of the dunghill."

Fine feathers don't make fine birds.

THE FOX AND
THE HEDGEHOG

A Fox swimming across a rapid river was carried by the force of the current into a very deep ravine, where he lay for a long time very much bruised, sick, and unable to move. A swarm of hungry blood-sucking flies settled upon him. A Hedgehog, passing by, saw his anguish and inquired if he should drive away the flies that were tormenting him. "By no means," replied the Fox; "pray do not molest them." "How is this?" said the Hedgehog; "do you not want to be rid of them?" "No," returned the Fox, "for these flies which you see are full of blood, and sting me but little, and if you rid me of these which are already satiated, others more hungry will come in their place, and will drink up all the blood I have left."

THE EAGLE, THE CAT, AND THE WILD SOW

An Eagle made her nest at the top of a lofty oak; a Cat, having found a convenient hole, moved into the middle of the trunk; and a Wild Sow, with her young, took shelter in a hollow at its foot. The Cat cunningly resolved to destroy this chance-made colony. To carry out her design, she climbed to the nest of the Eagle, and said, "Destruction is preparing for you, and for me too, unfortunately. The Wild Sow, whom you see daily digging up the earth, wishes to uproot the oak, so she may on its fall seize our families as food for her young." Having thus frightened the Eagle out of her senses, she crept down to the cave of the Sow, and said, "Your children are in great danger; for as soon as you go out with your litter to find food, the Eagle is prepared to pounce upon one of your little pigs." Having instilled these fears into the Sow, she went and pretended to hide herself in the hollow of the tree. When night came she went forth with silent foot and obtained food for herself and her kittens, but feigning to be afraid, she kept a lookout all through the day. Meanwhile, the Eagle, full of fear of the Sow, sat still on the branches, and the Sow, terrified by the Eagle, did not dare to go out from her cave. And thus they both, along with their families, perished from hunger, and afforded ample provision for the Cat and her kittens.

THE THIEF AND
THE INNKEEPER

A Thief hired a room in a tavern and stayed a while in the hope of stealing something which should enable him to pay his reckoning. When he had waited some days in vain, he saw the Innkeeper dressed in a new and handsome coat and sitting before his door. The Thief sat down beside him and talked with him. As the conversation began to flag, the Thief yawned terribly and at the same time howled like a wolf. The Innkeeper said, "Why do you howl so fearfully?" "I will tell you," said the Thief, "but first let me ask you to hold my clothes, or I shall tear them to pieces. I know not, sir, when I got this habit of yawning, nor whether these attacks of howling were inflicted on me as a judgment for my crimes, or for any other cause; but this I do know, that when I yawn for the third time, I actually turn into a wolf and attack men." With this speech he commenced a second fit of yawning and again howled like a wolf, as he had at first. The Innkeeper, hearing his tale and believing what he said, became greatly alarmed and, rising from his seat, attempted to run away. The Thief laid hold of his coat and entreated him to stop, saying, "Pray wait, sir, and hold my clothes, or I shall tear them to pieces in my fury, when I turn into a wolf." At the same moment he yawned the third time and set up a terrible howl.

The Innkeeper, frightened lest he should be attacked, left his new coat in the Thief's hand and ran as fast as he could into the inn for safety. The Thief made off with the coat and did not return again to the inn.

Every tale is not to be believed.

THE MULE

A Mule, frolicsome from lack of work and from too much corn, galloped about in a very extravagant manner, and said to himself: "My father surely was a high-mettled racer, and I am his own child in speed and spirit." On the next day, being driven a long journey, and feeling very wearied, he exclaimed in a disconsolate tone: "I must have made a mistake; my father, after all, could have been only an ass."

THE HART AND THE VINE

A Hart, hard pressed in the chase, hid himself beneath the large leaves of a Vine. The huntsmen, in their haste, overshot the place of his concealment. Supposing all danger to have passed, the Hart began to nibble the tendrils of the Vine. One of the huntsmen, attracted by the rustling of the leaves, looked back, and seeing the Hart, shot an arrow from his bow and struck it. The Hart, at the point of death, groaned: "I am rightly served, for I should not have maltreated the Vine that saved me."

THE SERPENT AND
THE EAGLE

A Serpent and an Eagle were struggling with each other in deadly conflict. The Serpent had the advantage, and was about to strangle the bird. A countryman saw them, and running up, loosed the coil of the Serpent and let the Eagle go free. The Serpent, irritated at the escape of his prey, injected his poison into the drinking horn of the countryman. The rustic, ignorant of his danger, was about to drink, when the Eagle struck his hand with his wing, and, seizing the drinking horn in his talons, carried it aloft.

THE CROW AND
THE PITCHER

A Crow perishing with thirst saw a pitcher, and hoping to find water, flew to it with delight. When he reached it, he discovered to his grief that it contained so little water that he could not possibly get at it. He tried everything he could think of to reach the water, but all his efforts were in vain. At last he collected as many stones as he could carry and dropped them one by one with his beak into the pitcher, until he brought the water within his reach and thus saved his life.

Necessity is the mother of invention.

THE TWO FROGS

Two Frogs were neighbors. One inhabited a deep pond, far removed from public view; the other lived in a gully containing little water, and traversed by a country road. The Frog that lived in the pond warned his friend to change his residence and entreated him to come and live with him, saying that he would enjoy greater safety from danger and more abundant food. The other refused, saying that he felt it so very hard to leave a place to which he had become accustomed. A few days afterwards a heavy wagon passed through the gully and crushed him to death under its wheels.

A willful man will have his way to his own hurt.

THE WOLF AND THE FOX

At one time a very large and strong Wolf was born among the wolves, who exceeded all his fellow-wolves in strength, size, and swiftness, so that they unanimously decided to call him "Lion". The Wolf, with a lack of sense proportioned to his enormous size, thought that they gave him this name in earnest, and, leaving his own race, consorted exclusively with the lions. An old sly Fox, seeing this, said, "May I never make myself so ridiculous as you do in your pride and self-conceit; for even though you have the size of a lion among wolves, in a herd of lions you are definitely a wolf."

THE WALNUT-TREE

A Walnut tree standing by the roadside bore an abundant crop of fruit. For the sake of the nuts, the passers-by broke its branches with stones and sticks. The Walnut-Tree piteously exclaimed, "O wretched me! that those whom I cheer with my fruit should repay me with these painful requitals!"

THE GNAT AND THE LION

A Gnat came and said to a Lion, "I do not in the least fear you, nor are you stronger than I am. For in what does your strength consist? You can scratch with your claws and bite with your teeth – so can a woman in her quarrels. I repeat that I am altogether more powerful than you; and if you doubt it, let us fight and see who will conquer." The Gnat, having sounded his horn, fastened himself upon the Lion and stung him on the nostrils and the parts of the face devoid of hair. While trying to crush him, the Lion tore himself with his claws, until he punished himself severely. The Gnat thus prevailed over the Lion, and, buzzing about in a song of triumph, flew away. But shortly afterwards he became entangled in the meshes of a cobweb and was eaten by a spider. He greatly lamented his fate, saying, "Woe is me! that I, who can wage war successfully with the hugest beasts, should perish myself from this spider, the most inconsiderable of insects!"

THE MONKEY AND
THE DOLPHIN

A Sailor, bound on a long voyage, took with him a Monkey to amuse him while on shipboard. As he sailed off the coast of Greece, a violent tempest arose in which the ship was wrecked and he, his Monkey, and all the crew were obliged to swim for their lives. A Dolphin saw the Monkey contending with the waves, and supposing him to be a man (whom he is always said to befriend), came and placed himself under him, to convey him on his back in safety to the shore. When the Dolphin arrived with his burden in sight of land not far from Athens, he asked the Monkey if he were an Athenian. The latter replied that he was, and that he was descended from one of the most noble families in that city. The Dolphin then inquired if he knew the Piraeus (the famous harbor of Athens). Supposing that a man was meant, the Monkey answered that he knew him very well and that he was an intimate friend. The Dolphin, indignant at these falsehoods, dipped the Monkey under the water and drowned him.

THE JACKDAW AND
THE DOVES

A Jackdaw, seeing some Doves in a cote abundantly provided with food, painted himself white and joined them in order to share their plentiful maintenance. The Doves, as long as he was silent, supposed him to be one of themselves and admitted him to their cote. But when one day he forgot himself and began to chatter, they discovered his true character and drove him forth, pecking him with their beaks. Failing to obtain food among the Doves, he returned to the Jackdaws. They too, not recognizing him on account of his color, expelled him from living with them. So desiring two ends, he obtained neither.

THE HORSE AND THE STAG

At one time the Horse had the plain entirely to himself. Then a Stag intruded into his domain and shared his pasture. The Horse, desiring to revenge himself on the stranger, asked a man if he were willing to help him in punishing the Stag. The man replied that if the Horse would receive a bit in his mouth and agree to carry him, he would contrive effective weapons against the Stag. The Horse consented and allowed the man to mount him. From that hour he found that instead of obtaining revenge on the Stag, he had enslaved himself to the service of man.

THE KID AND THE WOLF

A Kid, returning without protection from the pasture, was pursued by a Wolf. Seeing he could not escape, he turned round, and said: "I know, friend Wolf, that I must be your prey, but before I die I would ask of you one favor, that you will play me a tune to which I may dance." The Wolf complied, and while he was piping and the Kid was dancing, some hounds hearing the sound ran up and began chasing the Wolf. Turning to the Kid, he said, "It is just what I deserve; for I, who am only a butcher, should not have turned piper to please you."

THE PROPHET

A Wizard, sitting in the marketplace, was telling the fortunes of the passers-by when a person ran up in great haste, and announced to him that the doors of his house had been broken open and that all his goods were being stolen. He sighed heavily and hastened away as fast as he could run. A neighbor saw him running and said, "Oh! you fellow there! you say you can foretell the fortunes of others; how is it you did not foresee your own?"

THE FOX AND THE MONKEY

A Fox and a Monkey were traveling together on the same road. As they journeyed, they passed through a cemetery full of monuments. "All these monuments which you see," said the Monkey, "are erected in honor of my ancestors, who were in their day freedmen and citizens of great renown." The Fox replied, "You have chosen a most appropriate subject for your falsehoods, as I am sure none of your ancestors will be able to contradict you."

A false tale often betrays itself.

THE THIEF AND
THE HOUSEDOG

A Thief came in the night to break into a house. He brought with him several slices of meat in order to pacify the Housedog, so that he would not alarm his master by barking. As the Thief threw him the pieces of meat, the Dog said, "If you think to stop my mouth, you will be greatly mistaken. This sudden kindness at your hands will only make me more watchful, lest under these unexpected favors to myself, you have some private ends to accomplish for your own benefit, and for my master's injury."

THE MAN, THE HORSE,
THE OX, AND THE DOG

A Horse, Ox, and Dog, driven to great straits by the cold, sought shelter and protection from Man. He received them kindly, lighted a fire, and warmed them. He let the Horse make free with his oats, gave the Ox an abundance of hay, and fed the Dog with meat from his own table. Grateful for these favors, the animals determined to repay him to the best of their ability. For this purpose, they divided the term of his life between them, and each endowed one portion of it with the qualities which chiefly characterized himself. The Horse chose his earliest years and gave them his own attributes: hence every man is in his youth impetuous, headstrong, and obstinate in maintaining his own opinion. The Ox took under his patronage the next term of life, and therefore man in his middle age is fond of work, devoted to labor, and resolute to amass wealth and to husband his resources. The end of life was reserved for the Dog, wherefore the old man is often snappish, irritable, hard to please, and selfish, tolerant only of his own household, but averse to strangers and to all who do not administer to his comfort or to his necessities.

THE APES AND
THE TWO TRAVELERS

Two Men, one who always spoke the truth and the other who told nothing but lies, were traveling together and by chance came to the land of Apes. One of the Apes, who had raised himself to be king, commanded them to be seized and brought before him, that he might know what was said of him among men. He ordered at the same time that all the Apes be arranged in a long row on his right hand and on his left, and that a throne be placed for him, as was the custom among men. After these preparations he signified that the two men should be brought before him, and greeted them with this salutation: "What sort of a king do I seem to you to be, O strangers?" The Lying Traveler replied, "You seem to me a most mighty king." "And what is your estimate of those you see around me?" "These," he made answer, "are worthy companions of yourself, fit at least to be ambassadors and leaders of armies." The Ape and all his court, gratified with the lie, commanded that a handsome present be given to the flatterer. On this the Truthful Traveler thought to himself, "If so great a reward be given for a lie, with what gift may not I be rewarded, if, according to my custom, I tell the truth?" The Ape quickly turned to him. "And pray how do I and these my friends around me seem to you?" "Thou art," he said, "a most excellent Ape, and all these thy companions after thy example are excellent Apes too." The King of the Apes, enraged at hearing these truths, gave him over to the teeth and claws of his companions.

THE WOLF AND
THE SHEPHERD

A Wolf followed a flock of sheep for a long time and did not attempt to injure one of them. The Shepherd at first stood on his guard against him, as against an enemy, and kept a strict watch over his movements. But when the Wolf, day after day, kept in the company of the sheep and did not make the slightest effort to seize them, the Shepherd began to look upon him as a guardian of his flock rather than as a plotter of evil against it; and when occasion called him one day into the city, he left the sheep entirely in his charge. The Wolf, now that he had the opportunity, fell upon the sheep, and destroyed the greater part of the flock. When the Shepherd returned to find his flock destroyed, he exclaimed: "I have been rightly served; why did I trust my sheep to a Wolf?"

THE HARES AND THE LIONS

The Hares harangued the assembly, and argued that all should be equal. The Lions made this reply: "Your words, O Hares! are good; but they lack both claws and teeth such as we have."

THE LARK AND
HER YOUNG ONES

A Lark had made her nest in the early spring on the young green wheat. The brood had almost grown to their full strength and attained the use of their wings and the full plumage of their feathers, when the owner of the field, looking over his ripe crop, said, "The time has come when I must ask all my neighbors to help me with my harvest." One of the young Larks heard his speech and related it to his mother, inquiring of her to what place they should move for safety. "There is no occasion to move yet, my son," she replied; "the man who only sends to his friends to help him with his harvest is not really in earnest." The owner of the field came again a few days later and saw the wheat shedding the grain from excess of ripeness. He said, "I will come myself tomorrow with my laborers, and with as many reapers as I can hire, and will get in the harvest." The Lark on hearing these words said to her brood, "It is time now to be off, my little ones, for the man is in earnest this time; he no longer trusts his friends, but will reap the field himself."

Self-help is the best help.

THE FOX AND THE LION

When a Fox who had never yet seen a Lion, fell in with him by chance for the first time in the forest, he was so frightened that he nearly died with fear. On meeting him for the second time, he was still much alarmed, but not to the same extent as at first. On seeing him the third time, he so increased in boldness that he went up to him and commenced a familiar conversation with him.

Acquaintance softens prejudices.

THE WEASEL AND THE MICE

A Weasel, inactive from age and infirmities, was not able to catch mice as he once did. He therefore rolled himself in flour and lay down in a dark corner. A Mouse, supposing him to be food, leaped upon him, and was instantly caught and squeezed to death. Another perished in a similar manner, and then a third, and still others after them. A very old Mouse, who had escaped many a trap and snare, observed from a safe distance the trick of his crafty foe and said, "Ah! you that lie there, may you prosper just in the same proportion as you are what you pretend to be!"

THE BOY BATHING

A Boy bathing in a river was in danger of being drowned. He called out to a passing traveler for help, but instead of holding out a helping hand, the man stood by unconcernedly, and scolded the boy for his imprudence. "Oh, sir!" cried the youth, "pray help me now and scold me afterwards."

Counsel without help is useless.

THE ASS AND THE WOLF

An Ass feeding in a meadow saw a Wolf approaching to seize him, and immediately pretended to be lame. The Wolf, coming up, inquired the cause of his lameness. The Ass replied that passing through a hedge he had trod with his foot upon a sharp thorn. He requested that the Wolf pull it out, lest when he ate him it should injure his throat. The Wolf consented and lifted up the foot, and was giving his whole mind to the discovery of the thorn, when the Ass, with his heels, kicked his teeth into his mouth and galloped away. The Wolf, being thus fearfully mauled, said, "I am rightly served, for why did I attempt the art of healing, when my father only taught me the trade of a butcher?"

THE SELLER OF IMAGES

A certain Man made a wooden image of Mercury and offered it for sale. When no one appeared willing to buy it, in order to attract purchasers, he cried out that he had the statue to sell of a benefactor who bestowed wealth and helped to heap up riches. One of the bystanders said to him, "My good fellow, why do you sell him, being such a one as you describe, when you may yourself enjoy the good things he has to give?" "Why," he replied, "I am in need of immediate help, and he is wont to give his good gifts very slowly."

THE FOX AND THE GRAPES

A famished Fox saw some clusters of ripe black grapes hanging from a trellised vine. She resorted to all her tricks to get at them, but wearied herself in vain, for she could not reach them. At last she turned away, hiding her disappointment and saying: "The Grapes are sour, and not ripe as I thought."

THE MAN AND HIS WIFE

A Man had a Wife who made herself hated by all the members of his household. Wishing to find out if she had the same effect on the persons in her father's house, he made some excuse to send her home on a visit to her father. After a short time she returned, and when he inquired how she had got on and how the servants had treated her, she replied, "The herdsmen and shepherds cast on me looks of aversion." He said, "O Wife, if you were disliked by those who go out early in the morning with their flocks and return late in the evening, what must have been felt towards you by those with whom you passed the whole day!"

Straws show how the wind blows.

THE PEACOCK AND JUNO

The Peacock made complaint to Juno that, while the nightingale pleased every ear with his song, he himself no sooner opened his mouth than he became a laughingstock to all who heard him. The Goddess, to console him, said, "But you far excel in beauty and in size. The splendor of the emerald shines in your neck and you unfold a tail gorgeous with painted plumage." "But for what purpose have I," said the bird, "this dumb beauty so long as I am surpassed in song?" "The lot of each," replied Juno, "has been assigned by the will of the Fates—to thee, beauty; to the eagle, strength; to the nightingale, song; to the raven, favorable, and to the crow, unfavorable auguries. These are all contented with the endowments allotted to them."

THE HAWK AND
THE NIGHTINGALE

A Nightingale, sitting aloft upon an oak and singing according to his wont, was seen by a Hawk who, being in need of food, swooped down and seized him. The Nightingale, about to lose his life, earnestly begged the Hawk to let him go, saying that he was not big enough to satisfy the hunger of a Hawk who, if he wanted food, ought to pursue the larger birds. The Hawk, interrupting him, said: "I should indeed have lost my senses if I should let go food ready in my hand, for the sake of pursuing birds which are not yet even within sight."

THE DOG, THE COCK, AND THE FOX

A Dog and a Cock being great friends, agreed to travel together. At nightfall they took shelter in a thick wood. The Cock flying up, perched himself on the branches of a tree, while the Dog found a bed beneath in the hollow trunk. When the morning dawned, the Cock, as usual, crowed very loudly several times. A Fox heard the sound, and wishing to make a breakfast on him, came and stood under the branches, saying how earnestly he desired to make the acquaintance of the owner of so magnificent a voice. The Cock, suspecting his civilities, said: "Sir, I wish you would do me the favor of going around to the hollow trunk below me, and waking my porter, so that he may open the door and let you in." When the Fox approached the tree, the Dog sprang out and caught him, and tore him to pieces.

THE WOLF AND THE GOAT

A Wolf saw a Goat feeding at the summit of a steep precipice, where he had no chance of reaching her. He called to her and earnestly begged her to come lower down, lest she fall by some mishap; and he added that the meadows lay where he was standing, and that the herbage was most tender. She replied, "No, my friend, it is not for the pasture that you invite me, but for yourself, who are in want of food."

THE LION AND THE BULL

A Lion, greatly desiring to capture a Bull, and yet afraid to attack him on account of his great size, resorted to a trick to ensure his destruction. He approached the Bull and said, "I have slain a fine sheep, my friend; and if you will come home and partake of him with me, I shall be delighted to have your company." The Lion said this in the hope that, as the Bull was in the act of reclining to eat, he might attack him to advantage, and make his meal on him. The Bull, on approaching the Lion's den, saw the huge spits and giant caldrons, and no sign whatever of the sheep, and, without saying a word, quietly took his departure. The Lion inquired why he went off so abruptly without a word of salutation to his host, who had not given him any cause for offense. "I have reasons enough," said the Bull. "I see no indication whatever of your having slaughtered a sheep, while I do see very plainly every preparation for your dining on a bull."

THE GOAT AND THE ASS

A Man once kept a Goat and an Ass. The Goat, envying the Ass on account of his greater abundance of food, said, "How shamefully you are treated: at one time grinding in the mill, and at another carrying heavy burdens;" and he further advised him to pretend to be epileptic and fall into a ditch and so obtain rest. The Ass listened to his words, and falling into a ditch, was very much bruised. His master, sending for a leech, asked his advice. He bade him pour upon the wounds the lungs of a Goat. They at once killed the Goat, and so healed the Ass.

THE TOWN MOUSE AND
THE COUNTRY MOUSE

A Country Mouse invited a Town Mouse, an intimate friend, to pay him a visit and partake of his country fare. As they were on the bare plowlands, eating their wheat-stocks and roots pulled up from the hedgerow, the Town Mouse said to his friend, "You live here the life of the ants, while in my house is the horn of plenty. I am surrounded by every luxury, and if you will come with me, as I wish you would, you shall have an ample share of my dainties." The Country Mouse was easily persuaded, and returned to town with his friend. On his arrival, the Town Mouse placed before him bread, barley, beans, dried figs, honey, raisins, and, last of all, brought a dainty piece of cheese from a basket. The Country Mouse, being much delighted at the sight of such good cheer, expressed his satisfaction in warm terms and lamented his own hard fate. Just as they were beginning to eat, someone opened the door, and they both ran off squeaking, as fast as they could, to a hole so narrow that two could only find room in it by squeezing. They had scarcely begun their repast again when someone else entered to take something out of a cupboard, whereupon the two Mice, more frightened than before, ran away and hid themselves. At last the Country Mouse, almost famished, said to his friend: "Although you have prepared for me so dainty a feast, I must leave you to enjoy it by yourself. It is surrounded by too many dangers to please me. I prefer my bare plowlands and roots from the hedgerow, where I can live in safety, and without fear."

THE WOLF, THE FOX, AND THE APE

A Wolf accused a Fox of theft, but the Fox entirely denied the charge. An Ape undertook to adjudge the matter between them. When each had fully stated his case the Ape announced this sentence: "I do not think you, Wolf, ever lost what you claim; and I do believe you, Fox, to have stolen what you so stoutly deny."

The dishonest, if they act honestly, get no credit.

THE FLY AND
THE DRAUGHT-MULE

A Fly sat on the axle-tree of a chariot, and addressing the Draught-Mule said, "How slow you are! Why do you not go faster? See if I do not prick your neck with my sting." The Draught-Mule replied, "I do not heed your threats; I only care for him who sits above you, and who quickens my pace with his whip, or holds me back with the reins. Away, therefore, with your insolence, for I know well when to go fast, and when to go slow."

THE FISHERMEN

Some Fishermen were out trawling their nets. Perceiving them to be very heavy, they danced about for joy and supposed that they had taken a large catch. When they had dragged the nets to the shore they found but few fish: the nets were full of sand and stones, and the men were beyond measure cast down so much at the disappointment which had befallen them, but because they had formed such very different expectations. One of their company, an old man, said, "Let us cease lamenting, my mates, for, as it seems to me, sorrow is always the twin sister of joy; and it was only to be looked for that we, who just now were over-rejoiced, should next have something to make us sad."

THE LION AND
THE THREE BULLS

Three Bulls for a long time pastured together. A Lion lay in ambush in the hope of making them his prey, but was afraid to attack them while they kept together. Having at last by guileful speeches succeeded in separating them, he attacked them without fear as they fed alone, and feasted on them one by one at his own leisure.

Union is strength.

THE FOWLER AND
THE VIPER

A Fowler, taking his bird-lime and his twigs, went out to catch birds. Seeing a thrush sitting upon a tree, he wished to take it, and fitting his twigs to a proper length, watched intently, having his whole thoughts directed towards the sky. While thus looking upwards, he unknowingly trod upon a Viper asleep just before his feet. The Viper, turning about, stung him, and falling into a swoon, the man said to himself, "Woe is me! that while I purposed to hunt another, I am myself fallen unawares into the snares of death."

THE HORSE AND THE ASS

A Horse, proud of his fine trappings, met an Ass on the highway. The Ass, being heavily laden, moved slowly out of the way. "Hardly," said the Horse, "can I resist kicking you with my heels." The Ass held his peace, and made only a silent appeal to the justice of the gods. Not long afterwards the Horse, having become broken-winded, was sent by his owner to the farm. The Ass, seeing him drawing a dungcart, thus derided him: "Where, O boaster, are now all thy gay trappings, thou who are thyself reduced to the condition you so lately treated with contempt?"

THE FOX AND THE MASK

A Fox entered the house of an actor and, rummaging through all his properties, came upon a Mask, an admirable imitation of a human head. He placed his paws on it and said, "What a beautiful head! Yet it is of no value, as it entirely lacks brains."

THE GEESE AND
THE CRANES

The Geese and the Cranes were feeding in the same meadow, when a birdcatcher came to ensnare them in his nets. The Cranes, being light of wing, fled away at his approach; while the Geese, being slower of flight and heavier in their bodies, were captured.

THE BLIND MAN AND
THE WHELP

A Blind Man was accustomed to distinguishing different animals by touching them with his hands. The whelp of a Wolf was brought him, with a request that he would feel it, and say what it was. He felt it, and being in doubt, said: "I do not quite know whether it is the cub of a Fox, or the whelp of a Wolf, but this I know full well. It would not be safe to admit him to the sheepfold."

Evil tendencies are shown in early life.

THE DOGS AND THE FOX

Some Dogs, finding the skin of a lion, began to tear it in pieces with their teeth. A Fox, seeing them, said, "If this lion were alive, you would soon find out that his claws were stronger than your teeth."

It is easy to kick a man that is down.

THE COBBLER TURNED DOCTOR

A Cobbler unable to make a living by his trade and made desperate by poverty, began to practice medicine in a town in which he was not known. He sold a drug, pretending that it was an antidote to all poisons, and obtained a great name for himself by long-winded puffs and advertisements. When the Cobbler happened to fall sick himself of a serious illness, the Governor of the town determined to test his skill. For this purpose he called for a cup, and while filling it with water, pretended to mix poison with the Cobbler's antidote, commanding him to drink it on the promise of a reward. The Cobbler, under the fear of death, confessed that he had no knowledge of medicine, and was only made famous by the stupid clamors of the crowd. The Governor then called a public assembly and addressed the citizens: "Of what folly have you been guilty? You have not hesitated to entrust your heads to a man, whom no one could employ to make even the shoes for their feet."

THE WOLF AND THE HORSE

A Wolf coming out of a field of oats met a Horse and thus addressed him: "I would advise you to go into that field. It is full of fine oats, which I have left untouched for you, as you are a friend whom I would love to hear enjoying good eating." The Horse replied, "If oats had been the food of wolves, you would never have indulged your ears at the cost of your belly."

Men of evil reputation, when they perform a good deed, fail to get credit for it.

THE BROTHER AND
THE SISTER

A father had one son and one daughter, the former remarkable for his good looks, the latter for her extraordinary ugliness. While they were playing one day as children, they happened by chance to look together into a mirror that was placed on their mother's chair. The boy congratulated himself on his good looks; the girl grew angry, and could not bear the self-praises of her brother, interpreting all he said (and how could she do otherwise?) into reflection on herself. She ran off to her father, to be avenged on her brother, and spitefully accused him of having, as a boy, made use of that which belonged only to girls. The father embraced them both, and bestowing his kisses and affection impartially on each, said, "I wish you both would look into the mirror every day: you, my son, that you may not spoil your beauty by evil conduct; and you, my daughter, that you may make up for your lack of beauty by your virtues."

THE WASPS,
THE PARTRIDGES, AND
THE FARMER

The Wasps and the Partridges, overcome with thirst, came to a Farmer and besought him to give them some water to drink. They promised amply to repay him the favor which they asked. The Partridges declared that they would dig around his vines and make them produce finer grapes. The Wasps said that they would keep guard and drive off thieves with their stings. But the Farmer interrupted them, saying: "I have already two oxen, who, without making any promises, do all these things. It is surely better for me to give the water to them than to you."

THE CROW AND MERCURY

A Crow caught in a snare prayed to Apollo to release him, making a vow to offer some frankincense at his shrine. But when rescued from his danger, he forgot his promise. Shortly afterwards, again caught in a snare, he passed by Apollo and made the same promise to offer frankincense to Mercury. Mercury soon appeared and said to him, "O thou most base fellow? how can I believe thee, who hast disowned and wronged thy former patron?"

THE NORTH WIND AND
THE SUN

The North Wind and the Sun disputed as to which was the most powerful, and agreed that he should be declared the victor who could first strip a wayfaring man of his clothes. The North Wind first tried his power and blew with all his might, but the keener his blasts, the closer the Traveler wrapped his cloak around him, until at last, resigning all hope of victory, the Wind called upon the Sun to see what he could do. The Sun suddenly shone out with all his warmth. The Traveler no sooner felt his genial rays than he took off one garment after another, and at last, fairly overcome with heat, undressed and bathed in a stream that lay in his path.

Persuasion is better than force.

THE TWO MEN WHO WERE ENEMIES

Two men, deadly enemies to each other, were sailing in the same vessel. Determined to keep as far apart as possible, the one seated himself in the stem, and the other in the prow of the ship. A violent storm arose, and with the vessel in great danger of sinking, the one in the stern inquired of the pilot which of the two ends of the ship would go down first. On his replying that he supposed it would be the prow, the Man said, "Death would not be grievous to me, if I could only see my enemy die before me."

THE GAMECOCKS AND
THE PARTRIDGE

A Man had two Gamecocks in his poultry-yard. One day by chance he found a tame Partridge for sale. He purchased it and brought it home to be reared with his Gamecocks. When the Partridge was put into the poultry-yard, they struck at it and followed it about, so that the Partridge became grievously troubled and supposed that he was thus evilly treated because he was a stranger. Not long afterwards he saw the Cocks fighting together and not separating before one had well beaten the other. He then said to himself, "I shall no longer distress myself at being struck at by these Gamecocks, when I see that they cannot even refrain from quarreling with each other."

THE QUACK FROG

A Frog once upon a time came forth from his home in the marsh and proclaimed to all the beasts that he was a learned physician, skilled in the use of drugs and able to heal all diseases. A Fox asked him, "How can you pretend to prescribe for others, when you are unable to heal your own lame gait and wrinkled skin?"

THE LION, THE WOLF, AND THE FOX

A Lion, growing old, lay sick in his cave. All the beasts came to visit their king, except the Fox. The Wolf therefore, thinking that he had a capital opportunity, accused the Fox to the Lion of not paying any respect to him who had the rule over them all and of not coming to visit him. At that very moment the Fox came in and heard these last words of the Wolf. The Lion roaring out in a rage against him, the Fox sought an opportunity to defend himself and said, "And who of all those who have come to you have benefited you so much as I, who have traveled from place to place in every direction, and have sought and learnt from the physicians the means of healing you?" The Lion commanded him immediately to tell him the cure, when he replied, "You must flay a wolf alive and wrap his skin yet warm around you." The Wolf was at once taken and flayed; whereon the Fox, turning to him, said with a smile, "You should have moved your master not to ill, but to good, will."

THE DOG'S HOUSE

In the wintertime, a Dog curled up in as small a space as possible on account of the cold, determined to make himself a house. However when the summer returned again, he lay asleep stretched at his full length and appeared to himself to be of a great size. Now he considered that it would be neither an easy nor a necessary work to make himself such a house as would accommodate him.

THE WOLF AND THE LION

Roaming by the mountainside at sundown, a Wolf saw his own shadow become greatly extended and magnified, and he said to himself, "Why should I, being of such an immense size and extending nearly an acre in length, be afraid of the Lion? Ought I not to be acknowledged as King of all the collected beasts?" While he was indulging in these proud thoughts, a Lion fell upon him and killed him. He exclaimed with a too late repentance, "Wretched me! this overestimation of myself is the cause of my destruction."

THE BIRDS, THE BEASTS, AND THE BAT

The Birds waged war with the Beasts, and each were by turns the conquerors. A Bat, fearing the uncertain issues of the fight, always fought on the side which he felt was the strongest. When peace was proclaimed, his deceitful conduct was apparent to both combatants. Therefore being condemned by each for his treachery, he was driven forth from the light of day, and henceforth concealed himself in dark hiding-places, flying always alone and at night.

THE SPENDTHRIFT AND
THE SWALLOW

A Young Man, a great spendthrift, had run through all his patrimony and had but one good cloak left. One day he happened to see a Swallow, which had appeared before its season, skimming along a pool and twittering gaily. He supposed that summer had come, and went and sold his cloak. Not many days later, winter set in again with renewed frost and cold. When he found the unfortunate Swallow lifeless on the ground, he said, "Unhappy bird! what have you done? By thus appearing before the springtime you have not only killed yourself, but you have wrought my destruction also."

THE FOX AND THE LION

A Fox saw a Lion confined in a cage, and standing near him, bitterly reviled him. The Lion said to the Fox, "It is not thou who revilest me; but this mischance which has befallen me."

THE OWL AND THE BIRDS

An Owl, in her wisdom, counseled the Birds that when the acorn first began to sprout, to pull it all up out of the ground and not allow it to grow. She said acorns would produce mistletoe, from which an irremediable poison, the bird-lime, would be extracted and by which they would be captured. The Owl next advised them to pluck up the seed of the flax, which men had sown, as it was a plant which boded no good to them. And, lastly, the Owl, seeing an archer approach, predicted that this man, being on foot, would contrive darts armed with feathers which would fly faster than the wings of the Birds themselves. The Birds gave no credence to these warning words, but considered the Owl to be beside herself and said that she was mad. But afterwards, finding her words were true, they wondered at her knowledge and deemed her to be the wisest of birds. Hence it is that when she appears they look to her as knowing all things, while she no longer gives them advice, but in solitude laments their past folly.

THE TRUMPETER TAKEN PRISONER

A Trumpeter, bravely leading on the soldiers, was captured by the enemy. He cried out to his captors, "Pray spare me, and do not take my life without cause or without inquiry. I have not slain a single man of your troop. I have no arms, and carry nothing but this one brass trumpet." "That is the very reason for which you should be put to death," they said; "for, while you do not fight yourself, your trumpet stirs all the others to battle."

THE ASS IN
THE LION'S SKIN

An Ass, having put on the Lion's skin, roamed about in the forest and amused himself by frightening all the foolish animals he met in his wanderings. At last coming upon a Fox, he tried to frighten him also, but the Fox no sooner heard the sound of his voice than he exclaimed, "I might possibly have been frightened myself, if I had not heard your bray."

THE SPARROW AND
THE HARE

A Hare pounced upon by an eagle sobbed very much and uttered cries like a child. A Sparrow upbraided her and said, "Where now is thy remarkable swiftness of foot? Why were your feet so slow?" While the Sparrow was thus speaking, a hawk suddenly seized him and killed him. The Hare was comforted in her death, and expiring said, "Ah! you who so lately, when you supposed yourself safe, exulted over my calamity, have now reason to deplore a similar misfortune."

THE FLEA AND THE OX

A Flea thus questioned an Ox: "What ails you, that being so huge and strong, you submit to the wrongs you receive from men and slave for them day by day, while I, being so small a creature, mercilessly feed on their flesh and drink their blood without stint?" The Ox replied: "I do not wish to be ungrateful, for I am loved and well cared for by men, and they often pat my head and shoulders." "Woe's me!" said the Flea; "this very patting which you like, whenever it happens to me, brings with it my inevitable destruction."

THE GOODS AND THE ILLS

All the Goods were once driven out by the Ills from that common share which they each had in the affairs of mankind; for the Ills by reason of their numbers had prevailed to possess the earth. The Goods wafted themselves to heaven and asked for a righteous vengeance on their persecutors. They entreated Jupiter that they might no longer be associated with the Ills, as they had nothing in common and could not live together, but were engaged in unceasing warfare; and that an indissoluble law might be laid down for their future protection. Jupiter granted their request and decreed that henceforth the Ills should visit the earth in company with each other, but that the Goods should one by one enter the habitations of men. Hence it arises that Ills abound, for they come not one by one, but in troops, and by no means singly: while the Goods proceed from Jupiter, and are given, not alike to all, but singly, and separately; and one by one to those who are able to discern them.

THE DOVE AND THE CROW

A Dove shut up in a cage was boasting of the large number of young ones which she had hatched. A Crow hearing her, said: "My good friend, cease from this unseasonable boasting. The larger the number of your family, the greater your cause of sorrow, in seeing them shut up in this prison-house."

MERCURY AND
THE WORKMEN

A Workman, felling wood by the side of a river, let his axe drop by accident into a deep pool. Being thus deprived of the means of his livelihood, he sat down on the bank and lamented his hard fate. Mercury appeared and demanded the cause of his tears. After he told him his misfortune, Mercury plunged into the stream, and, bringing up a golden axe, inquired if that were the one he had lost. On his saying that it was not his, Mercury disappeared beneath the water a second time, returned with a silver axe in his hand, and again asked the Workman if it were his. When the Workman said it was not, he dived into the pool for the third time and brought up the axe that had been lost. The Workman claimed it and expressed his joy at its recovery. Mercury, pleased with his honesty, gave him the golden and silver axes in addition to his own. The Workman, on his return to his house, related to his companions all that had happened. One of them at once resolved to try and secure the same good fortune for himself. He ran to the river and threw his axe on purpose into the pool at the same place, and sat down on the bank to weep. Mercury appeared to him just as he hoped he would; and having learned the cause of his grief, plunged into the stream and brought up a golden axe, inquiring if he had lost it. The Workman seized it greedily, and declared that truly it was the very same axe that he had lost. Mercury, displeased at his knavery, not only took away the golden axe, but refused to recover for him the axe he had thrown into the pool.

THE EAGLE AND
THE JACKDAW

An Eagle, flying down from his perch on a lofty rock, seized upon a lamb and carried him aloft in his talons. A Jackdaw, who witnessed the capture of the lamb, was stirred with envy and determined to emulate the strength and flight of the Eagle. He flew around with a great whir of his wings and settled upon a large ram, with the intention of carrying him off, but his claws became entangled in the ram's fleece and he was not able to release himself, although he fluttered with his feathers as much as he could. The Shepherd, seeing what had happened, ran up and caught him. He at once clipped the Jackdaw's wings, and taking him home at night, gave him to his children. On their saying, "Father, what kind of bird is it?" he replied, "To my certain knowledge he is a Daw; but he would like you to think an Eagle."

THE FOX AND THE CRANE

A Fox invited a Crane to supper and provided nothing for his entertainment but some soup made of pulse, which was poured out into a broad flat stone dish. The soup fell out of the long bill of the Crane at every mouthful, and his vexation at not being able to eat afforded the Fox much amusement. The Crane, in his turn, asked the Fox to sup with him, and set before her a flagon with a long narrow mouth, so that he could easily insert his neck and enjoy its contents at his leisure. The Fox, unable even to taste it, met with a fitting requital, after the fashion of her own hospitality.

JUPITER, NEPTUNE, MINERVA, AND MOMUS

According to an ancient legend, the first man was made by Jupiter, the first bull by Neptune, and the first house by Minerva. On the completion of their labors, a dispute arose as to which had made the most perfect work. They agreed to appoint Momus as judge, and to abide by his decision. Momus, however, being very envious of the handicraft of each, found fault with all. He first blamed the work of Neptune because he had not made the horns of the bull below his eyes, so he might better see where to strike. He then condemned the work of Jupiter, because he had not placed the heart of man on the outside, that everyone might read the thoughts of the evil disposed and take precautions against the intended mischief. And, lastly, he inveighed against Minerva because she had not contrived iron wheels in the foundation of her house, so its inhabitants might more easily remove if a neighbor proved unpleasant. Jupiter, indignant at such inveterate faultfinding, drove him from his office of judge, and expelled him from the mansions of Olympus.

THE EAGLE AND THE FOX

An Eagle and a Fox formed an intimate friendship and decided to live near each other. The Eagle built her nest in the branches of a tall tree, while the Fox crept into the underwood and there produced her young. Not long after they had agreed upon this plan, the Eagle, being in want of provision for her young ones, swooped down while the Fox was out, seized upon one of the little cubs, and feasted herself and her brood. The Fox on her return, discovered what had happened, but was less grieved for the death of her young than for her inability to avenge them. A just retribution, however, quickly fell upon the Eagle. While hovering near an altar, on which some villagers were sacrificing a goat, she suddenly seized a piece of the flesh, and carried it, along with a burning cinder, to her nest. A strong breeze soon fanned the spark into a flame, and the eaglets, as yet unfledged and helpless, were roasted in their nest and dropped down dead at the bottom of the tree. There, in the sight of the Eagle, the Fox gobbled them up.

THE MAN AND THE SATYR

A Man and a Satyr once drank together in token of a bond of alliance being formed between them. One very cold wintry day, as they talked, the Man put his fingers to his mouth and blew on them. When the Satyr asked the reason for this, he told him that he did it to warm his hands because they were so cold. Later on in the day they sat down to eat, and the food prepared was quite scalding. The Man raised one of the dishes a little towards his mouth and blew in it. When the Satyr again inquired the reason, he said that he did it to cool the meat, which was too hot. "I can no longer consider you as a friend," said the Satyr, "a fellow who with the same breath blows hot and cold."

THE ASS AND
HIS PURCHASER

A Man wished to purchase an Ass, and agreed with its owner that he should try out the animal before he bought him. He took the Ass home and put him in the straw-yard with his other Asses, upon which the new animal left all the others and at once joined the one that was most idle and the greatest eater of them all. Seeing this, the Man put a halter on him and led him back to his owner. On being asked how, in so short a time, he could have made a trial of him, he answered, "I do not need a trial; I know that he will be just the same as the one he chose for his companion."

A man is known by the company he keeps.

THE TWO BAGS

Every man, according to an ancient legend, is born into the world with two bags suspended from his neck – a small bag in front full of his neighbors' faults, and a large bag behind filled with his own faults. Hence it is that men are quick to see the faults of others, and yet are often blind to their own failings.

THE STAG AT THE POOL

A Stag overpowered by heat came to a spring to drink. Seeing his own shadow reflected in the water, he greatly admired the size and variety of his horns, but felt angry with himself for having such slender and weak feet. While he was thus contemplating himself, a Lion appeared at the pool and crouched to spring upon him. The Stag immediately took to flight, and exerting his utmost speed, as long as the plain was smooth and open kept himself easily at a safe distance from the Lion. But entering a wood he became entangled by his horns, and the Lion quickly came up to him and caught him. When too late, he thus reproached himself: "Woe is me! How I have deceived myself! These feet which would have saved me I despised, and I gloried in these antlers which have proved my destruction."

What is most truly valuable is often underrated.

THE JACKDAW AND
THE FOX

A half-famished Jackdaw seated himself on a fig-tree, which had produced some fruit entirely out of season, and waited in the hope that the figs would ripen. A Fox seeing him sitting so long and learning the reason of his doing so, said to him, "You are indeed, sir, sadly deceiving yourself; you are indulging a hope strong enough to cheat you, but which will never reward you with enjoyment."

THE LARK BURYING
HER FATHER

The Lark (according to an ancient legend) was created before the earth itself, and when her father died, as there was no earth, she could find no place of burial for him. She let him lie uninterred for five days, and on the sixth day, not knowing what else to do, she buried him in her own head. Hence she obtained her crest, which is popularly said to be her father's grave-hillock.

Youth's first duty is reverence to parents.

THE GNAT AND THE BULL

A Gnat settled on the horn of a Bull, and sat there a long time. Just as he was about to fly off, he made a buzzing noise, and inquired of the Bull if he would like him to go. The Bull replied, "I did not know you had come, and I shall not miss you when you go away."

Some men are of more consequence in their own eyes than in the eyes of their neighbors.

THE BITCH AND
HER WHELPS

A Bitch, ready to whelp, earnestly begged a shepherd for a place where she might litter. When her request was granted, she besought permission to rear her puppies in the same spot. The shepherd again consented. But at last the Bitch, protected by the bodyguard of her whelps, who had now grown up and were able to defend themselves, asserted her exclusive right to the place and would not permit the shepherd to approach.

THE DOGS AND THE HIDES

Some Dogs famished with hunger saw a number of cowhides steeping in a river. Not being able to reach them, they agreed to drink up the river, but it happened that they burst themselves with drinking long before they reached the hides.

Attempt not impossibilities.

THE SHEPHERD AND
THE SHEEP

A Shepherd driving his Sheep to a wood, saw an oak of unusual size full of acorns, and spreading his cloak under the branches, he climbed up into the tree and shook them down. The Sheep eating the acorns inadvertently frayed and tore the cloak. When the Shepherd came down and saw what was done, he said, "O you most ungrateful creatures! You provide wool to make garments for all other men, but you destroy the clothes of him who feeds you."

THE GRASSHOPPER AND
THE OWL

An Owl, accustomed to feed at night and to sleep during the day, was greatly disturbed by the noise of a Grasshopper and earnestly besought her to stop chirping. The Grasshopper refused to desist, and chirped louder and louder the more the Owl entreated. When she saw that she could get no redress and that her words were despised, the Owl attacked the chatterer by a stratagem. "Since I cannot sleep," she said, "on account of your song which, believe me, is sweet as the lyre of Apollo, I shall indulge myself in drinking some nectar which Pallas lately gave me. If you do not dislike it, come to me and we will drink it together." The Grasshopper, who was thirsty, and pleased with the praise of her voice, eagerly flew up. The Owl came forth from her hollow, seized her, and put her to death.

THE MONKEY AND
THE CAMEL

The Beasts of the forest gave a splendid entertainment at which the Monkey stood up and danced. Having vastly delighted the assembly, he sat down amidst universal applause. The Camel, envious of the praises bestowed on the Monkey and desiring to divert to himself the favor of the guests, proposed to stand up in his turn and dance for their amusement. He moved about in so utterly ridiculous a manner that the Beasts, in a fit of indignation, set upon him with clubs and drove him out of the assembly.

It is absurd to ape our betters.

THE PEASANT AND
THE APPLE-TREE

A Peasant had in his garden an Apple-tree which bore no fruit but only served as a harbor for the sparrows and grasshoppers. He resolved to cut it down, and taking his axe in his hand, made a bold stroke at its roots. The grasshoppers and sparrows entreated him not to cut down the tree that sheltered them, but to spare it, and they would sing to him and lighten his labors. He paid no attention to their request, but gave the tree a second and a third blow with his axe. When he reached the hollow of the tree, he found a hive full of honey. Having tasted the honeycomb, he threw down his axe, and looking on the tree as sacred, took great care of it.

Self-interest alone moves some men.

THE TWO SOLDIERS AND
THE ROBBER

Two Soldiers traveling together were set upon by a Robber. The one fled away; the other stood his ground and defended himself with his stout right hand. The Robber being slain, the timid companion ran up and drew his sword, and then, throwing back his traveling cloak said, "I'll at him, and I'll take care he shall learn whom he has attacked." On this, he who had fought with the Robber made answer, "I only wish that you had helped me just now, even if it had been only with those words, for I should have been the more encouraged, believing them to be true; but now put up your sword in its sheath and hold your equally useless tongue, till you can deceive others who do not know you. I, indeed, who have experienced with what speed you run away, know right well that no dependence can be placed on your valor."

THE TREES UNDER
THE PROTECTION OF
THE GODS

The Gods, according to an ancient legend, made choice of certain trees to be under their special protection. Jupiter chose the oak, Venus the myrtle, Apollo the laurel, Cybele the pine, and Hercules the poplar. Minerva, wondering why they had preferred trees not yielding fruit, inquired the reason for their choice. Jupiter replied, "It is lest we should seem to covet the honor for the fruit." But said Minerva, "Let anyone say what he will, the olive is more dear to me on account of its fruit." Then said Jupiter, "My daughter, you are rightly called wise; for unless what we do is useful, the glory of it is vain."

THE MOTHER AND
THE WOLF

A famished Wolf was prowling about in the morning in search of food. As he passed the door of a cottage built in the forest, he heard a Mother say to her child, "Be quiet, or I will throw you out of the window, and the Wolf shall eat you." The Wolf sat all day waiting at the door. In the evening he heard the same woman fondling her child and saying: "You are quiet now, and if the Wolf should come, we will kill him." The Wolf, hearing these words, went home, gasping with cold and hunger. When he reached his den, Mistress Wolf inquired of him why he returned wearied and supperless, so contrary to his wont. He replied: "Why, forsooth! use I gave credence to the words of a woman!"

THE ASS AND THE HORSE

An Ass besought a Horse to spare him a small portion of his feed. "Yes," said the Horse; "if any remains out of what I am now eating I will give it you for the sake of my own superior dignity, and if you will come when I reach my own stall in the evening, I will give you a little sack full of barley." The Ass replied, "Thank you. But I can't think that you, who refuse me a little matter now, will by and by confer on me a greater benefit."

TRUTH AND THE TRAVELER

A wayfaring Man, traveling in the desert, met a Woman standing alone and terribly dejected. He inquired of her, "Who art thou?" "My name is Truth," she replied. "And for what cause," he asked, "have you left the city to dwell alone here in the wilderness?" She made answer, "Because in former times, falsehood was with few, but is now with all men."

THE MANSLAYER

A Man committed a murder, and was pursued by the relations of the man whom he murdered. On his reaching the river Nile he saw a Lion on its bank and being fearfully afraid, climbed up a tree. He found a Serpent in the upper branches of the tree, and again being greatly alarmed, he threw himself into the river, where a Crocodile caught him and ate him. Thus the earth, the air, and the water alike refused shelter to a murderer.

THE LION AND THE FOX

A Fox entered into partnership with a Lion on the pretense of becoming his servant. Each undertook his proper duty in accordance with his own nature and powers. The Fox discovered and pointed out the prey; the Lion sprang on it and seized it. The Fox soon became jealous of the Lion carrying off the Lion's share, and said that he would no longer find out the prey, but would capture it on his own account. The next day he attempted to snatch a lamb from the fold, but he himself fell prey to the huntsmen and hounds.

THE LION AND THE EAGLE

An Eagle stayed his flight and entreated a Lion to make an alliance with him to their mutual advantage. The Lion replied, "I have no objection, but you must excuse me for requiring you to find surety for your good faith, for how can I trust anyone as a friend who is able to fly away from his bargain whenever he pleases?"

Try before you trust.

THE HEN AND
THE SWALLOW

A Hen finding the eggs of a viper and carefully keeping them warm, nourished them into life. A Swallow, observing what she had done, said, "You silly creature! why have you hatched these vipers which, when they shall have grown, will inflict injury on all, beginning with yourself?"

THE BUFFOON AND
THE COUNTRYMAN

A rich Nobleman once opened the theaters without charge to the people, and gave a public notice that he would handsomely reward any person who invented a new amusement for the occasion. Various public performers contended for the prize. Among them came a Buffoon well known among the populace for his jokes, and said that he had a kind of entertainment which had never been brought out on any stage before. This report being spread about made a great stir, and the theater was crowded in every part. The Buffoon appeared alone upon the platform, without any apparatus or confederates, and the very sense of expectation caused an intense silence. He suddenly bent his head towards his bosom and imitated the squeaking of a little pig so admirably with his voice that the audience declared he had a porker under his cloak, and demanded that it should be shaken out. When that was done and nothing was found, they cheered the actor, and loaded him with the loudest applause. A Countryman in the crowd, observing all that has passed, said, "So help me, Hercules, he shall not beat me at that trick!" and at once proclaimed that he would do the same thing on the next day, though in a much more natural way. On the morrow a still larger crowd assembled in the theater, but now partiality for their favorite actor very generally prevailed, and the audience came rather to ridicule the Countryman than to see the spectacle. Both of the performers appeared on the stage. The Buffoon grunted and squeaked away first, and obtained, as on the preceding day, the applause and cheers of the spectators. Next the Countryman commenced, and pretending that he concealed a little pig beneath his clothes (which in truth he did, but not suspected by the audience) contrived to take hold of and to pull his ear causing the pig to squeak. The crowd, however, cried out with one consent that the Buffoon had given a far more exact imitation, and clamored for the Countryman to be kicked out of the theater. On this the rustic produced the little pig from his cloak and showed by the most positive proof the greatness of their mistake. "Look here," he said, "this shows what sort of judges you are."

THE CROW AND
THE SERPENT

A Crow in great want of food saw a Serpent asleep in a sunny nook, and flying down, greedily seized him. The Serpent, turning about, bit the Crow with a mortal wound. In the agony of death, the bird exclaimed: "O unhappy me! who have found in that which I deemed a happy windfall the source of my destruction."

THE HUNTER AND
THE HORSEMAN

A certain Hunter, having snared a hare, placed it upon his shoulders and set out homewards. On his way he met a man on horseback who begged the hare of him, under the pretense of purchasing it. However, when the Horseman got the hare, he rode off as fast as he could. The Hunter ran after him, as if he was sure of overtaking him, but the Horseman increased more and more the distance between them. The Hunter, sorely against his will, called out to him and said, "Get along with you! for I will now make you a present of the hare."

THE KING'S SON AND
THE PAINTED LION

A King, whose only son was fond of martial exercises, had a dream in which he was warned that his son would be killed by a lion. Afraid the dream should prove true, he built for his son a pleasant palace and adorned its walls for his amusement with all kinds of life-sized animals, among which was the picture of a lion. When the young Prince saw this, his grief at being thus confined burst out afresh, and, standing near the lion, he said: "O you most detestable of animals! through a lying dream of my father's, which he saw in his sleep, I am shut up on your account in this palace as if I had been a girl: what shall I now do to you?" With these words he stretched out his hands toward a thorn-tree, meaning to cut a stick from its branches so that he might beat the lion. But one of the tree's prickles pierced his finger and caused great pain and inflammation, so that the young Prince fell down in a fainting fit. A violent fever suddenly set in, from which he died not many days later.

We had better bear our troubles bravely than try to escape them.

THE CAT AND VENUS

A Cat fell in love with a handsome young man, and entreated Venus to change her into the form of a woman. Venus consented to her request and transformed her into a beautiful damsel, so that the youth saw her and loved her, and took her home as his bride. While the two were reclining in their chamber, Venus wishing to discover if the Cat in her change of shape had also altered her habits of life, let down a mouse in the middle of the room. The Cat, quite forgetting her present condition, started up from the couch and pursued the mouse, wishing to eat it. Venus was much disappointed and again caused her to return to her former shape.

Nature exceeds nurture.

THE SHE-GOATS AND
THEIR BEARDS

The She-goats having obtained a beard by request to Jupiter, the He-Goats were sorely displeased and made complaint that the females equaled them in dignity. "Allow them," said Jupiter, "to enjoy an empty honor and to assume the badge of your nobler sex, so long as they are not your equals in strength or courage."

It matters little if those who are inferior to us in merit should be like us in outside appearances.

THE CAMEL AND THE ARAB

An arab Camel-driver, after completing the loading of his Camel, asked him which he would like best, to go up hill or down. The poor beast replied, not without a touch of reason: "Why do you ask me? Is it that the level way through the desert is closed?"

THE MILLER, HIS SON, AND THEIR ASS

A Miller and his son were driving their Ass to a neighboring fair to sell him. They had not gone far when they met with a troop of women collected round a well, talking and laughing. "Look there," cried one of them, "did you ever see such fellows, to be trudging along the road on foot when they might ride?" The old man hearing this, quickly made his son mount the Ass, and continued to walk along merrily by his side. Presently they came up to a group of old men in earnest debate. "There," said one of them, "it proves what I was a-saying. What respect is shown to old age in these days? Do you see that idle lad riding while his old father has to walk? Get down, you young scapegrace, and let the old man rest his weary limbs." Upon this the old man made his son dismount, and got up himself. In this manner they had not proceeded far when they met a company of women and children: "Why, you lazy old fellow," cried several tongues at once, "how can you ride upon the beast, while that poor little lad there can hardly keep pace by the side of you?" The good-natured Miller immediately took up his son behind him. They had now almost reached the town. "Pray, honest friend," said a citizen, "is that Ass your own?" "Yes," replied the old man. "O, one would not have thought so," said the other, "by the way you load him. Why, you two fellows are better able to carry the poor beast than he you." "Anything to please you," said the old man; "we can but try." So, alighting with his son, they tied the legs of the Ass together and with the help of a pole endeavored to carry him on their shoulders over a bridge near the entrance to the town. This entertaining sight brought the people in crowds to laugh at it, till the Ass, not liking the noise nor the strange handling that he was subject to, broke the cords that bound him and, tumbling off the pole, fell into the river. Upon this, the old man, vexed and ashamed, made the best of his way home again, convinced that by endeavoring to please everybody he had pleased nobody, and lost his Ass in the bargain.

THE CROW AND THE SHEEP

A troublesome Crow seated herself on the back of a Sheep. The Sheep, much against his will, carried her backward and forward for a long time, and at last said, "If you had treated a dog in this way, you would have had your deserts from his sharp teeth." To this the Crow replied, "I despise the weak and yield to the strong. I know whom I may bully and whom I must flatter; and I thus prolong my life to a good old age."

THE FOX AND
THE BRAMBLE

A Fox was mounting a hedge when he lost his footing and caught hold of a Bramble to save himself. Having pricked and grievously torn the soles of his feet, he accused the Bramble because, when he had fled to her for assistance, she had used him worse than the hedge itself. The Bramble, interrupting him, said, "But you really must have been out of your senses to fasten yourself on me, who am myself always accustomed to fasten upon others."

THE WOLF AND THE LION

A Wolf, having stolen a lamb from a fold, was carrying him off to his lair. A Lion met him in the path, and seizing the lamb, took it from him. Standing at a safe distance, the Wolf exclaimed, "You have unrighteously taken that which was mine from me!" To which the Lion jeeringly replied, "It was righteously yours, eh? The gift of a friend?"

THE DOG AND THE OYSTER

A Dog, used to eating eggs, saw an Oyster and, opening his mouth to its widest extent, swallowed it down with the utmost relish, supposing it to be an egg. Soon afterwards suffering great pain in his stomach, he said, "I deserve all this torment, for my folly in thinking that everything round must be an egg."

They who act without sufficient thought, will often fall into unsuspected danger.

THE ANT AND THE DOVE

An Ant went to the bank of a river to quench its thirst, and being carried away by the rush of the stream, was on the point of drowning. A Dove sitting on a tree overhanging the water plucked a leaf and let it fall into the stream close to her. The Ant climbed onto it and floated in safety to the bank. Shortly afterwards a birdcatcher came and stood under the tree, and laid his lime-twigs for the Dove, which sat in the branches. The Ant, perceiving his design, stung him in the foot. In pain the birdcatcher threw down the twigs, and the noise made the Dove take wing.

THE PARTRIDGE AND
THE FOWLER

A Fowler caught a Partridge and was about to kill it. The Partridge earnestly begged him to spare his life, saying, "Pray, master, permit me to live and I will entice many Partridges to you in recompense for your mercy to me." The Fowler replied, "I shall now with less scruple take your life, because you are willing to save it at the cost of betraying your friends and relations."

THE FLEA AND THE MAN

A Man, very much annoyed with a Flea, caught him at last, and said, "Who are you who dare to feed on my limbs, and to cost me so much trouble in catching you?" The Flea replied, "O my dear sir, pray spare my life, and destroy me not, for I cannot possibly do you much harm." The Man, laughing, replied, "Now you shall certainly die by mine own hands, for no evil, whether it be small or large, ought to be tolerated."

THE THIEVES AND
THE COCK

Some Thieves broke into a house and found nothing but a Cock, whom they stole, and got off as fast as they could. Upon arriving at home they prepared to kill the Cock, who thus pleaded for his life: "Pray spare me; I am very serviceable to men. I wake them up in the night to their work." "That is the very reason why we must the more kill you," they replied; "for when you wake your neighbors, you entirely put an end to our business."

The safeguards of virtue are hateful to those with evil intentions.

THE DOG AND THE COOK

A rich Man gave a great feast, to which he invited many friends and acquaintances. His Dog availed himself of the occasion to invite a stranger Dog, a friend of his, saying, "My master gives a feast, and there is always much food remaining; come and sup with me tonight." The Dog thus invited went at the hour appointed, and seeing the preparations for so grand an entertainment, said in the joy of his heart, "How glad I am that I came! I do not often get such a chance as this. I will take care and eat enough to last me both today and tomorrow." While he was congratulating himself and wagging his tail to convey his pleasure to his friend, the Cook saw him moving about among his dishes and, seizing him by his fore and hind paws, bundled him without ceremony out of the window. He fell with force upon the ground and limped away, howling dreadfully. His yelling soon attracted other street dogs, who came up to him and inquired how he had enjoyed his supper. He replied, "Why, to tell you the truth, I drank so much wine that I remember nothing. I do not know how I got out of the house."

THE TRAVELERS AND
THE PLANE-TREE

Two Travelers, worn out by the heat of the summer's sun, laid themselves down at noon under the widespreading branches of a Plane-tree. As they rested under its shade, one of the Travelers said to the other, "What a singularly useless tree is the Plane! It bears no fruit, and is not of the least service to man." The Plane-tree, interrupting him, said, "You ungrateful fellows! Do you, while receiving benefits from me and resting under my shade, dare to describe me as useless, and unprofitable?"

Some men underrate their best blessings.

THE HARES AND
THE FROGS

The Hares, oppressed by their own exceeding timidity and weary of the perpetual alarm to which they were exposed, with one accord determined to put an end to themselves and their troubles by jumping from a lofty precipice into a deep lake below. As they scampered off in large numbers to carry out their resolve, the Frogs lying on the banks of the lake heard the noise of their feet and rushed helter-skelter to the deep water for safety. On seeing the rapid disappearance of the Frogs, one of the Hares cried out to his companions: "Stay, my friends, do not do as you intended; for you now see that there are creatures who are still more timid than ourselves."

THE LION, JUPITER, AND THE ELEPHANT

The Lion wearied Jupiter with his frequent complaints. "It is true, O Jupiter!" he said, "that I am gigantic in strength, handsome in shape, and powerful in attack. I have jaws well provided with teeth, and feet furnished with claws, and I lord it over all the beasts of the forest, and what a disgrace it is, that being such as I am, I should be frightened by the crowing of a cock." Jupiter replied, "Why do you blame me without a cause? I have given you all the attributes which I possess myself, and your courage never fails you except in this one instance." On hearing this the Lion groaned and lamented very much and, reproaching himself with his cowardice, wished that he might die. As these thoughts passed through his mind, he met an Elephant and came close to hold a conversation with him. After a time he observed that the Elephant shook his ears very often, and he inquired what was the matter and why his ears moved with such a tremor every now and then. Just at that moment a Gnat settled on the head of the Elephant, and he replied, "Do you see that little buzzing insect? If it enters my ear, my fate is sealed. I should die presently." The Lion said, "Well, since so huge a beast is afraid of a tiny gnat, I will no more complain, nor wish myself dead. I find myself, even as I am, better off than the Elephant."

THE LAMB AND THE WOLF

A Wolf pursued a Lamb, which fled for refuge to a certain Temple. The Wolf called out to him and said, "The Priest will slay you in sacrifice, if he should catch you." On which the Lamb replied, "It would be better for me to be sacrificed in the Temple than to be eaten by you."

THE RICH MAN AND
THE TANNER

A rich Man lived near a Tanner, and not being able to bear the unpleasant smell of the tan-yard, he pressed his neighbor to go away. The Tanner put off his departure from time to time, saying that he would leave soon. But as he still continued to stay, as time went on, the rich Man became accustomed to the smell, and feeling no manner of inconvenience, made no further complaints.

THE SHIPWRECKED MAN
AND THE SEA

A shipwrecked Man, having been cast upon a certain shore, slept after his buffetings with the deep. After a while he awoke, and looking upon the Sea, loaded it with reproaches. He argued that it enticed men with the calmness of its looks, but when it had induced them to plow its waters, it grew rough and destroyed them. The Sea, assuming the form of a woman, replied to him: "Blame not me, my good sir, but the winds, for I am by my own nature as calm and firm even as this earth; but the winds suddenly falling on me create these waves, and lash me into fury."

THE MULES AND
THE ROBBERS

Two Mules well-laden with packs were trudging along. One carried panniers filled with money, the other sacks weighted with grain. The Mule carrying the treasure walked with head erect, as if conscious of the value of his burden, and tossed up and down the clear-toned bells fastened to his neck. His companion followed with quiet and easy step. All of a sudden Robbers rushed upon them from their hiding-places, and in the scuffle with their owners, wounded with a sword the Mule carrying the treasure, which they greedily seized while taking no notice of the grain. The Mule which had been robbed and wounded bewailed his misfortunes. The other replied, "I am indeed glad that I was thought so little of, for I have lost nothing, nor am I hurt with any wound."

THE VIPER AND THE FILE

A Lion, entering the workshop of a smith, sought from the tools the means of satisfying his hunger. He more particularly addressed himself to a File, and asked of him the favor of a meal. The File replied, "You must indeed be a simple-minded fellow if you expect to get anything from me, who am accustomed to take from everyone, and never to give anything in return."

THE LION AND
THE SHEPHERD

A Lion, roaming through a forest, trod upon a thorn. Soon afterward he came up to a Shepherd and fawned upon him, wagging his tail as if to say, "I am a suppliant, and seek your aid." The Shepherd boldly examined the beast, discovered the thorn, and placing his paw upon his lap, pulled it out; thus relieved of his pain, the Lion returned into the forest. Some time after, the Shepherd, being imprisoned on a false accusation, was condemned "to be cast to the Lions" as the punishment for his imputed crime. But when the Lion was released from his cage, he recognized the Shepherd as the man who healed him, and instead of attacking him, approached and placed his foot upon his lap. The King, as soon as he heard the tale, ordered the Lion to be set free again in the forest, and the Shepherd to be pardoned and restored to his friends.

THE CAMEL AND JUPITER

The Camel, when he saw the Bull adorned with horns, envied him and wished that he himself could obtain the same honors. He went to Jupiter, and besought him to give him horns. Jupiter, vexed at his request because he was not satisfied with his size and strength of body, and desired yet more, not only refused to give him horns, but even deprived him of a portion of his ears.

THE PANTHER AND
THE SHEPHERDS

A Panther, by some mischance, fell into a pit. The Shepherds discovered him, and some threw sticks at him and pelted him with stones, while others, moved with compassion towards one about to die even though no one should hurt him, threw in some food to prolong his life. At night they returned home, not dreaming of any danger, but supposing that on the morrow they would find him dead. The Panther, however, when he had recruited his feeble strength, freed himself with a sudden bound from the pit, and hastened to his den with rapid steps. After a few days he came forth and slaughtered the cattle, and, killing the Shepherds who had attacked him, raged with angry fury. Then they who had spared his life, fearing for their safety, surrendered to him their flocks and begged only for their lives. To them the Panther made this reply: "I remember alike those who sought my life with stones, and those who gave me food aside, therefore, your fears. I return as an enemy only to those who injured me."

THE ASS AND
THE CHARGER

An Ass congratulated a Horse on being so ungrudgingly and carefully provided for, while he himself had scarcely enough to eat and not even that without hard work. But when war broke out, a heavily armed soldier mounted the Horse, and riding him to the charge, rushed into the very midst of the enemy. The Horse was wounded and fell dead on the battle-field. Then the Ass, seeing all these things, changed his mind, and commiserated the Horse.

THE EAGLE AND
HIS CAPTOR

An Eagle was once captured by a Man, who immediately clipped his wings and put him into his poultry-yard with the other birds, at which treatment the Eagle was weighed down with grief. Later, another neighbor purchased him and allowed his feathers to grow again. The Eagle took flight, and pouncing upon a Hare, brought it at once as an offering to his benefactor. A Fox, seeing this, exclaimed, "Do not cultivate the favor of this man, but of your former owner, lest he should again hunt for you and deprive you a second time of your wings."

THE BALD MAN AND THE FLY

A Fly bit the bare head of a Bald Man who, endeavoring to destroy it, gave himself a heavy slap. Escaping, the Fly said mockingly, "You who have wished to revenge, even with death, the prick of a tiny insect, see what you have done to yourself to add insult to injury?" The Bald Man replied, "I can easily make peace with myself, because I know there was no intention to hurt. But you, an ill-favored and contemptible insect who delights in sucking human blood, I wish that I could have killed you even if I had incurred a heavier penalty."

THE OLIVE-TREE AND
THE FIG-TREE

The Olive-tree ridiculed the Fig-tree because, while she was green all the year round, the Fig-tree changed its leaves with the seasons. A shower of snow fell upon them, and, finding the Olive full of foliage, it settled upon its branches and broke them down with its weight, at once despoiling it of its beauty and killing the tree. But finding the Fig-tree denuded of leaves, the snow fell through to the ground, and did not injure it at all.

THE EAGLE AND THE KITE

An Eagle, overwhelmed with sorrow, sat upon the branches of a tree in company with a Kite. "Why," said the Kite, "do I see you with such a rueful look?" "I seek," she replied, "a mate suitable for me, and am not able to find one." "Take me," returned the Kite, "I am much stronger than you are." "Why, are you able to secure the means of living by your plunder?" "Well, I have often caught and carried away an ostrich in my talons." The Eagle, persuaded by these words, accepted him as her mate. Shortly after the nuptials, the Eagle said, "Fly off and bring me back the ostrich you promised me." The Kite, soaring aloft into the air, brought back the shabbiest possible mouse, stinking from the length of time it had lain about the fields. "Is this," said the Eagle, "the faithful fulfillment of your promise to me?" The Kite replied, "That I might attain your royal hand, there is nothing that I would not have promised, however much I knew that I must fail in the performance."

THE ASS AND HIS DRIVER

An Ass, being driven along a high road, suddenly started off and bolted to the brink of a deep precipice. While he was in the act of throwing himself over, his owner seized him by the tail, endeavoring to pull him back. When the Ass persisted in his effort, the man let him go and said, "Conquer, but conquer to your cost."

THE THRUSH AND
THE FOWLER

A Thrush was feeding on a myrtle-tree and did not move from it because its berries were so delicious. A Fowler observed her staying so long in one spot, and having well bird-limed his reeds, caught her. The Thrush, being at the point of death, exclaimed, "O foolish creature that I am! For the sake of a little pleasant food I have deprived myself of my life."

THE ROSE AND THE AMARANTH

An Amaranth planted in a garden near a Rose-tree, thus addressed it: "What a lovely flower is the Rose, a favorite alike with Gods and with men. I envy you your beauty and your perfume." The Rose replied, "I indeed, dear Amaranth, flourish but for a brief season! If no cruel hand pluck me from my stem, yet I must perish by an early doom. But thou art immortal and dost never fade, but bloomest for ever in renewed youth."

THE FROGS' COMPLAINT AGAINST THE SUN

Once upon a time, when the Sun announced his intention to take a wife, the Frogs lifted up their voices in clamor to the sky. Jupiter, disturbed by the noise of their croaking, inquired the cause of their complaint. One of them said, "The Sun, now while he is single, parches up the marsh, and compels us to die miserably in our arid homes. What will be our future condition if he should beget other suns?"

CLASSIC LITERATURE: WORDS AND PHRASES
adapted from the Collins English Dictionary

Accoucheur NOUN a male midwife or doctor ❑ *I think my sister must have had some general idea that I was a young offender whom an Accoucheur Policemen had taken up (on my birthday) and delivered over to her* (*Great Expectations* by Charles Dickens)

addled ADJ confused and unable to think properly ❑ *But she counted and counted till she got that addled* (*The Adventures of Huckleberry Finn* by Mark Twain)

admiration NOUN amazement or wonder ❑ *lifting up his hands and eyes by way of admiration* (*Gulliver's Travels* by Jonathan Swift)

afeard ADJ afeard means afraid ❑ *shake it – and don't be afeard* (*The Adventures of Huckleberry Finn* by Mark Twain)

affected VERB affected means followed ❑ *Hadst thou affected sweet divinity* (*Doctor Faustus 5.2* by Christopher Marlowe)

aground ADV when a boat runs aground, it touches the ground in a shallow part of the water and gets stuck ❑ *what kep' you? – boat get aground?* (*The Adventures of Huckleberry Finn* by Mark Twain)

ague NOUN a fever in which the patient has alternate hot and cold shivering fits ❑ *his exposure to the wet and cold had brought on fever and ague* (*Oliver Twist* by Charles Dickens)

alchemy ADJ false or worthless ❑ *all wealth alchemy* (*The Sun Rising* by John Donne)

all alike PHRASE the same all the time ❑ *Love, all alike* (*The Sun Rising* by John Donne)

alow and aloft PHRASE alow means in the lower part or bottom, and aloft means on the top, so alow and aloft means on the top and in the bottom or throughout ❑ *Someone's turned the chest out alow and aloft* (*Treasure Island* by Robert Louis Stevenson)

ambuscade NOUN ambuscade is not a proper word. Tom means an ambush, which is when a group of people attack their enemies, after hiding and waiting for them ❑ *and so we would lie in ambuscade, as he called it* (*The Adventures of Huckleberry Finn* by Mark Twain)

amiable ADJ likeable or pleasant ❑ *Such amiable qualities must speak for themselves* (*Pride and Prejudice* by Jane Austen)

amulet NOUN an amulet is a charm thought to drive away evil spirits. ❑ *uttered phrases at once occult and familiar, like the amulet worn on the heart* (*Silas Marner* by George Eliot)

amusement NOUN here amusement means a strange and disturbing puzzle ❑ *this was an amusement the other way* (*Robinson Crusoe* by Daniel Defoe)

ancient NOUN an ancient was the flag displayed on a ship to show which country it belongs to. It is also called the ensign ❑ *her ancient and pendants out* (*Robinson Crusoe* by Daniel Defoe)

antic ADJ here antic means horrible or grotesque ❑ *armed and dressed after a very antic manner* (*Gulliver's Travels* by Jonathan Swift)

antics NOUN antics is an old word meaning clowns, or people who do silly things to make other people laugh ❑ *And point like antics at his triple crown* (*Doctor Faustus 3.2* by Christopher Marlowe)

appanage NOUN an appanage is a living allowance ❑ *As if loveliness were not the special prerogative of woman – her legitimate appanage and heritage!* (*Jane Eyre* by Charlotte Brontë)

appended VERB appended means attached or added to ❑ *and these words appended* (*Treasure Island* by Robert Louis Stevenson)

approver NOUN an approver is someone who gives evidence against someone he used to work with ❑ *Mr. Noah Claypole: receiving a free pardon from the Crown in consequence of being admitted approver against Fagin* (*Oliver Twist* by Charles Dickens)

areas NOUN the areas is the space, below street level, in front of the basement of a house ❑ *The Dodger had a vicious propensity, too, of pulling the caps from the heads of small boys and tossing them down areas* (*Oliver Twist* by Charles Dickens)

argument NOUN theme or important idea or subject which runs through a piece of writing ❑ *Thrice needful to the argument which now* (*The Prelude* by William Wordsworth) .

artificially ADJ artfully or cleverly ❑ *and he with a sharp flint sharpened very artificially* (*Gulliver's Travels* by Jonathan Swift)

artist NOUN here artist means a skilled workman ❑ *This man was a most ingenious artist* (*Gulliver's Travels* by Jonathan Swift)

assizes NOUN assizes were regular court sessions which a visiting judge was in charge of ❑ *you shall hang at the next assizes* (*Treasure Island* by Robert Louis Stevenson)

attraction NOUN gravitation, or Newton's theory of gravitation ❑ *he predicted the same fate to attraction* (*Gulliver's Travels* by Jonathan Swift)

aver VERB to aver is to claim something strongly ❑ *for Jem Rodney,*

the mole catcher, averred that one evening as he was returning homeward (*Silas Marner* by George Eliot)

baby NOUN here baby means doll, which is a child's toy that looks like a small person ❑ *and skilful dressing her baby* (*Gulliver's Travels* by Jonathan Swift)

bagatelle NOUN bagatelle is a game rather like billiards and pool ❑ *Breakfast had been ordered at a pleasant little tavern, a mile or so away upon the rising ground beyond the green; and there was a bagatelle board in the room, in case we should desire to unbend our minds after the solemnity.* (*Great Expectations* by Charles Dickens)

bah EXCLAM Bah is an exclamation of frustration or anger ❑ *"Bah," said Scrooge.* (*A Christmas Carol* by Charles Dickens)

bairn NOUN a northern word for child ❑ *Who has taught you those fine words, my bairn?* (*Wuthering Heights* by Emily Brontë)

bait VERB to bait means to stop on a journey to take refreshment ❑ *So, when they stopped to bait the horse, and ate and drank and enjoyed themselves, I could touch nothing that they touched, but kept my fast unbroken.* (*David Copperfield* by Charles Dickens)

balustrade NOUN a balustrade is a row of vertical columns that form railings ❑ *but I mean to say you might have got a hearse up that staircase, and taken it broadwise, with the splinter-bar towards the wall, and the door towards the balustrades: and done it easy* (*A Christmas Carol* by Charles Dickens)

bandbox NOUN a large lightweight box for carrying bonnets or hats ❑ *I am glad I bought my bonnet, if it is only for the fun of having another bandbox* (*Pride and Prejudice* by Jane Austen)

barren NOUN a barren here is a stretch or expanse of barren land ❑ *a line* of upright stones, continued the length of the barren (*Wuthering Heights* by Emily Brontë)

basin NOUN a basin was a cup without a handle ❏ *who is drinking his tea out of a basin* (*Wuthering Heights* by Emily Brontë)

battalia NOUN the order of battle ❏ *till I saw part of his army in battalia* (*Gulliver's Travels* by Jonathan Swift)

battery NOUN a Battery is a fort or a place where guns are positioned ❏ *You bring the lot to me, at that old Battery over yonder* (*Great Expectations* by Charles Dickens)

battledore and shuttlecock NOUN The game battledore and shuttlecock was an early version of the game now known as badminton. The aim of the early game was simply to keep the shuttlecock from hitting the ground. ❏ *Battledore and shuttlecock's a wery good game vhen you an't the shuttlecock and two lawyers the battledores, in which case it gets too excitin' to be pleasant* (*Pickwick Papers* by Charles Dickens)

beadle NOUN a beadle was a local official who had power over the poor ❏ *But these impertinences were speedily checked by the evidence of the surgeon, and the testimony of the beadle* (*Oliver Twist* by Charles Dickens)

bearings NOUN the bearings of a place are the measurements or directions that are used to find or locate it ❏ *the bearings of the island* (*Treasure Island* by Robert Louis Stevenson)

beaufet NOUN a beaufet was a sideboard ❏ *and sweet-cake from the beaufet* (*Emma* by Jane Austen)

beck NOUN a beck is a small stream ❏ *a beck which follows the bend of the glen* (*Wuthering Heights* by Emily Brontë)

bedight VERB decorated ❏ *and bedight with Christmas holly stuck into the top.* (*A Christmas Carol* by Charles Dickens)

Bedlam NOUN Bedlam was a lunatic asylum in London which had statues carved by Caius Gabriel Cibber at its entrance ❏ *Bedlam, and those carved maniacs at the gates* (*The Prelude* by William Wordsworth)

beeves NOUN oxen or castrated bulls which are animals used for pulling vehicles or carrying things ❏ *to deliver in every morning six beeves* (*Gulliver's Travels* by Jonathan Swift)

begot VERB created or caused ❏ *Begot in thee* (*On His Mistress* by John Donne)

behoof NOUN behoof means benefit ❏ *"Yes, young man," said he, releasing the handle of the article in question, retiring a step or two from my table, and speaking for the behoof of the landlord and waiter at the door* (*Great Expectations* by Charles Dickens)

berth NOUN a berth is a bed on a boat ❏ *this is the berth for me* (*Treasure Island* by Robert Louis Stevenson)

bevers NOUN a bever was a snack, or small portion of food, eaten between main meals ❏ *that buys me thirty meals a day and ten bevers* (*Doctor Faustus 2.1* by Christopher Marlowe)

bilge water NOUN the bilge is the widest part of a ship's bottom, and the bilge water is the dirty water that collects there ❏ *no gush of bilge-water had turned it to fetid puddle* (*Jane Eyre* by Charlotte Brontë)

bills NOUN bills is an old term meaning prescription. A prescription is the piece of paper on which your doctor writes an order for medicine and which you give to a chemist to get the medicine ❏ *Are not thy bills hung up as monuments* (*Doctor Faustus 1.1* by Christopher Marlowe)

black cap NOUN a judge wore a black cap when he was about to sentence a prisoner to death ❏ *The judge* assumed the black cap, and the prisoner still stood with the same air and gesture. (*Oliver Twist* by Charles Dickens)

boot-jack NOUN a wooden device to help take boots off ❑ *The speaker appeared to throw a boot-jack, or some such article, at the person he addressed* (*Oliver Twist* by Charles Dickens)

booty NOUN booty means treasure or prizes ❑ *would be inclined to give up their booty in payment of the dead man's debts* (*Treasure Island* by Robert Louis Stevenson)

Bow Street runner PHRASE Bow Street runners were the first British police force, set up by the author Henry Fielding in the eighteenth century ❑ *as would have convinced a judge or a Bow Street runner* (*Treasure Island* by Robert Louis Stevenson)

brawn NOUN brawn is a dish of meat which is set in jelly ❑ *Heaped up upon the floor, to form a kind of throne, were turkeys, geese, game, poultry, brawn, great joints of meat, sucking-pigs* (*A Christmas Carol* by Charles Dickens)

bray VERB when a donkey brays, it makes a loud, harsh sound ❑ *and she doesn't bray like a jackass* (*The Adventures of Huckleberry Finn* by Mark Twain)

break VERB in order to train a horse you first have to break it ❑ *"If a high-mettled creature like this," said he, "can't be broken by fair means, she will never be good for anything"* (*Black Beauty* by Anna Sewell)

bullyragging VERB bullyragging is an old word which means bullying. To bullyrag someone is to threaten or force someone to do something they don't want to do ❑ *and a lot of loafers bullyragging him for sport* (*The Adventures of Huckleberry Finn* by Mark Twain)

but PREP except for (this) ❑ *but this, all pleasures fancies be* (*The Good-Morrow* by John Donne)

by hand PHRASE by hand was a common expression of the time meaning that baby had been fed either using a spoon or a bottle rather than by breast-feeding ❑ *My sister, Mrs. Joe Gargery, was more than twenty years older than I, and had established a great reputation with herself . . . because she had bought me up 'by hand'* (*Great Expectations* by Charles Dickens)

bye-spots NOUN bye-spots are lonely places ❑ *and bye-spots of tales rich with indigenous produce* (*The Prelude* by William Wordsworth)

calico NOUN calico is plain white fabric made from cotton ❑ *There was two old dirty calico dresses* (*The Adventures of Huckleberry Finn* by Mark Twain)

camp-fever NOUN camp-fever was another word for the disease typhus ❑ *during a severe camp-fever* (*Emma* by Jane Austen)

cant NOUN cant is insincere or empty talk ❑ *"Man," said the Ghost, "if man you be in heart, not adamant, forbear that wicked cant until you have discovered What the surplus is, and Where it is."* (*A Christmas Carol* by Charles Dickens)

canty ADJ canty means lively, full of life ❑ *My mother lived til eighty, a canty dame to the last* (*Wuthering Heights* by Emily Brontë)

canvas VERB to canvas is to discuss ❑ *We think so very differently on this point Mr Knightley, that there can be no use in canvassing it* (*Emma* by Jane Austen)

capital ADJ capital means excellent or extremely good ❑ *for it's capital, so shady, light, and big* (*Little Women* by Louisa May Alcott)

capstan NOUN a capstan is a device used on a ship to lift sails and anchors ❑ *capstans going, ships going out to sea, and unintelligible sea creatures roaring curses over the bulwarks at respondent* lightermen (*Great Expectations* by Charles Dickens)

case-bottle NOUN a square bottle designed to fit with others into a case ❑ *The spirit being set before him in a huge case-bottle, which had originally come out of some ship's locker* (*The Old Curiosity Shop* by Charles Dickens)

casement NOUN casement is a word meaning window. The teacher in Nicholas Nickleby misspells window showing what a bad teacher he is ❑ *W-i-n, win, d-e-r, der, winder, a casement.'* (*Nicholas Nickleby* by Charles Dickens)

cataleptic ADJ a cataleptic fit is one in which the victim goes into a trance-like state and remains still for a long time ❑ *It was at this point in their history that Silas's cataleptic fit occurred during the prayer-meeting* (*Silas Marner* by George Eliot)

cauldron NOUN a cauldron is a large cooking pot made of metal ❑ *stirring a large cauldron which seemed to be full of soup* (*Alice's Adventures in Wonderland* by Lewis Carroll)

cephalic ADJ cephalic means to do with the head ❑ *with ink composed of a cephalic tincture* (*Gulliver's Travels* by Jonathan Swift)

chaise and four NOUN a closed four-wheel carriage pulled by four horses ❑ *he came down on Monday in a chaise and four to see the place* (*Pride and Prejudice* by Jane Austen)

chamberlain NOUN the main servant in a household ❑ *In those times a bed was always to be got there at any hour of the night, and the chamberlain, letting me in at his ready wicket, lighted the candle next in order on his shelf* (*Great Expectations* by Charles Dickens)

characters NOUN distinguishing marks ❑ *Impressed upon all forms the characters* (*The Prelude* by William Wordsworth)

chary ADJ cautious ❑ *I should have been chary of discussing my guardian too freely even with her* (*Great Expectations* by Charles Dickens)

cherishes VERB here cherishes means cheers or brightens ❑ *some philosophic song of Truth that cherishes our daily life* (*The Prelude* by William Wordsworth)

chickens' meat PHRASE chickens' meat is an old term which means chickens' feed or food ❑ *I had shook a bag of chickens' meat out in that place* (*Robinson Crusoe* by Daniel Defoe)

chimeras NOUN a chimera is an unrealistic idea or a wish which is unlikely to be fulfilled ❑ *with many other wild impossible chimeras* (*Gulliver's Travels* by Jonathan Swift)

chines NOUN chine is a cut of meat that includes part or all of the backbone of the animal ❑ *and they found hams and chines uncut* (*Silas Marner* by George Eliot)

chits NOUN chits is a slang word which means girls ❑ *I hate affected, niminy-piminy chits!* (*Little Women* by Louisa May Alcott)

chopped VERB chopped means come suddenly or accidentally ❑ *if I had chopped upon them* (*Robinson Crusoe* by Daniel Defoe)

chute NOUN a narrow channel ❑ *One morning about day-break, I found a canoe and crossed over a chute to the main shore* (*The Adventures of Huckleberry Finn* by Mark Twain)

circumspection NOUN careful observation of events and circumstances; caution ❑ *I honour your circumspection* (*Pride and Prejudice* by Jane Austen)

clambered VERB clambered means to climb somewhere with difficulty, usually using your hands and your feet ❑ *he clambered up and down stairs* (*Treasure Island* by Robert Louis Stevenson)

clime NOUN climate ❏ *no season knows nor clime* (*The Sun Rising* by John Donne)

clinched VERB clenched ❏ *the tops whereof I could but just reach with my fist clinched* (*Gulliver's Travels* by Jonathan Swift)

close chair NOUN a close chair is a sedan chair, which is an covered chair which has room for one person. The sedan chair is carried on two poles by two men, one in front and one behind ❏ *persuaded even the Empress herself to let me hold her in her close chair* (*Gulliver's Travels* by Jonathan Swift)

clown NOUN clown here means peasant or person who lives off the land ❏ *In ancient days by emperor and clown* (*Ode on a Nightingale* by John Keats)

coalheaver NOUN a coalheaver loaded coal onto ships using a spade ❏ *Good, strong, wholesome medicine, as was given with great success to two Irish labourers and a coalheaver* (*Oliver Twist* by Charles Dickens)

coal-whippers NOUN men who worked at docks using machines to load coal onto ships ❏ *here, were colliers by the score and score, with the coal-whippers plunging off stages on deck* (*Great Expectations* by Charles Dickens)

cobweb NOUN a cobweb is the net which a spider makes for catching insects ❏ *the walls and ceilings were all hung round with cobwebs* (*Gulliver's Travels* by Jonathan Swift)

coddling VERB coddling means to treat someone too kindly or protect them too much ❏ *and I've been coddling the fellow as if I'd been his grandmother* (*Little Women* by Louisa May Alcott)

coil NOUN coil means noise or fuss or disturbance ❏ *What a coil is there?* (*Doctor Faustus 4.7* by Christopher Marlowe)

collared VERB to collar something is a slang term which means to capture. In this sentence, it means he stole it [the money] ❏ *he collared it* (*The Adventures of Huckleberry Finn* by Mark Twain)

colling VERB colling is an old word which means to embrace and kiss ❏ *and no clasping and colling at all* (*Tess of the D'Urbervilles* by Thomas Hardy)

colloquies NOUN colloquy is a formal conversation or dialogue ❏ *Such colloquies have occupied many a pair of pale-faced weavers* (*Silas Marner* by George Eliot)

comfit NOUN sugar-covered pieces of fruit or nut eaten as sweets ❏ *and pulled out a box of comfits* (*Alice's Adventures in Wonderland* by Lewis Carroll)

coming out VERB when a girl came out in society it meant she was of marriageable age. In order to 'come out' girls were expecting to attend balls and other parties during a season ❏ *The younger girls formed hopes of coming out a year or two sooner than they might otherwise have done* (*Pride and Prejudice* by Jane Austen)

commit VERB commit means arrest or stop ❏ *Commit the rascals* (*Doctor Faustus 4.7* by Christopher Marlowe)

commodious ADJ commodious means convenient ❏ *the most commodious and effectual ways* (*Gulliver's Travels* by Jonathan Swift)

commons NOUN commons is an old term meaning food shared with others ❏ *his pauper assistants ranged themselves behind him; the gruel was served out; and a long grace was said over the short commons.* (*Oliver Twist* by Charles Dickens)

complacency NOUN here complacency means a desire to please others. Today complacency means feeling pleased with oneself without good reason. ❏ *Twas thy power that raised the first complacency in me* (*The Prelude* by William Wordsworth)

complaisance NOUN complaisance was eagerness to please ❏ *we cannot wonder at his complaisance* (Pride and Prejudice by Jane Austen)

complaisant ADJ complaisant means polite ❏ *extremely cheerful and complaisant to their guest* (Gulliver's Travels by Jonathan Swift)

conning VERB conning means learning by heart ❏ *Or conning more* (The Prelude by William Wordsworth)

consequent NOUN consequence ❏ *as avarice is the necessary consequent of old age* (Gulliver's Travels by Jonathan Swift)

consorts NOUN concerts ❏ *The King, who delighted in music, had frequent consorts at Court* (Gulliver's Travels by Jonathan Swift)

conversible ADJ conversible meant easy to talk to, companionable ❏ *He can be a conversible companion* (Pride and Prejudice by Jane Austen)

copper NOUN a copper is a large pot that can be heated directly over a fire ❏ *He gazed in stupefied astonishment on the small rebel for some seconds, and then clung for support to the copper* (Oliver Twist by Charles Dickens)

copper-stick NOUN a copper-stick is the long piece of wood used to stir washing in the copper (or boiler) which was usually the biggest cooking pot in the house ❏ *It was Christmas Eve, and I had to stir the pudding for next day, with a copper-stick, from seven to eight by the Dutch clock* (Great Expectations by Charles Dickens)

counting-house NOUN a counting house is a place where accountants work ❏ *Once upon a time – of all the good days in the year, on Christmas Eve – old Scrooge sat busy in his countinghouse* (A Christmas Carol by Charles Dickens)

courtier NOUN a courtier is someone who attends the king or queen – a member of the court ❏ *next the ten courtiers;* (Alice's Adventures in Wonderland by Lewis Carroll)

covies NOUN covies were flocks of partridges ❏ *and will save all of the best covies for you* (Pride and Prejudice by Jane Austen)

cowed VERB cowed means frightened or intimidated ❏ *it cowed me more than the pain* (Treasure Island by Robert Louis Stevenson)

cozened VERB cozened means tricked or deceived ❏ *Do you remember, sir, how you cozened me* (Doctor Faustus 4.7 by Christopher Marlowe)

cravats NOUN a cravat is a folded cloth that a man wears wrapped around his neck as a decorative item of clothing ❏ *we'd'a' slept in our cravats to-night* (The Adventures of Huckleberry Finn by Mark Twain)

crock and dirt PHRASE crock and dirt is an old expression meaning soot and dirt ❏ *and the mare catching cold at the door, and the boy grimed with crock and dirt* (Great Expectations by Charles Dickens)

crockery NOUN here crockery means pottery ❏ *By one of the parrots was a cat made of crockery* (The Adventures of Huckleberry Finn by Mark Twain)

crooked sixpence PHRASE it was considered unlucky to have a bent sixpence ❏ *You've got the beauty, you see, and I've got the luck, so you must keep me by you for your crooked sixpence* (Silas Marner by George Eliot)

croquet NOUN croquet is a traditional English summer game in which players try to hit wooden balls through hoops ❏ *and once she remembered trying to box her own ears for having cheated herself in a game of croquet* (Alice's Adventures in Wonderland by Lewis Carroll)

cross PREP across ❏ *The two great streets, which run cross and divide it into four quarters* (Gulliver's Travels by Jonathan Swift)

329

culpable ADJ if you are culpable for something it means you are to blame ❑ *deep are the sorrows that spring from false ideas for which no man is culpable. (Silas Marner by George Eliot)*

cultured ADJ cultivated ❑ *Nor less when spring had warmed the cultured Vale (The Prelude by William Wordsworth)*

cupidity NOUN cupidity is greed ❑ *These people hated me with the hatred of cupidity and disappointment. (Great Expectations by Charles Dickens)*

curricle NOUN an open two-wheeled carriage with one seat for the driver and space for a single passenger ❑ *and they saw a lady and a gentleman in a curricle (Pride and Prejudice by Jane Austen)*

cynosure NOUN a cynosure is something that strongly attracts attention or admiration ❑ *Then I thought of Eliza and Georgiana; I beheld one the cynosure of a ballroom, the other the inmate of a convent cell (Jane Eyre by Charlotte Brontë)*

dalliance NOUN someone's dalliance with something is a brief involvement with it ❑ *nor sporting in the dalliance of love (Doctor Faustus Chorus by Christopher Marlowe)*

darkling ADV darkling is an archaic way of saying in the dark ❑ *Darkling I listen (Ode on a Nightingale by John Keats)*

delf-case NOUN a sideboard for holding dishes and crockery ❑ *at the pewter dishes and delf-case (Wuthering Heights by Emily Brontë)*

determined ■ VERB here determined means ended ❑ *and be out of vogue when that was determined (Gulliver's Travels by Jonathan Swift)* ■ VERB determined can mean to have been learned or found especially by investigation or experience ❑ *All the sensitive feelings it wounded so cruelly, all the shame and misery it kept alive within my breast, became more poignant as I thought of this; and I determined that the life was unendurable (David Copperfield by Charles Dickens)*

Deuce NOUN a slang term for the Devil ❑ *Ah, I dare say I did. Deuce take me, he added suddenly, I know I did. I find I am not quite unscrewed yet. (Great Expectations by Charles Dickens)*

diabolical ADJ diabolical means devilish or evil ❑ *and with a thousand diabolical expressions (Treasure Island by Robert Louis Stevenson)*

direction NOUN here direction means address ❑ *Elizabeth was not surprised at it, as Jane had written the direction remarkably ill (Pride and Prejudice by Jane Austen)*

discover VERB to make known or announce ❑ *the Emperor would discover the secret while I was out of his power (Gulliver's Travels by Jonathan Swift)*

dissemble VERB hide or conceal ❑ *Dissemble nothing (On His Mistress by John Donne)*

dissolve VERB dissolve here means to release from life, to die ❑ *Fade far away, dissolve, and quite forget (Ode on a Nightingale by John Keats)*

distrain VERB to distrain is to seize the property of someone who is in debt in compensation for the money owed ❑ *for he's threatening to distrain for it (Silas Marner by George Eliot)*

Divan NOUN a Divan was originally a Turkish council of state – the name was transferred to the couches they sat on and is used to mean this in English ❑ *Mr Brass applauded this picture very much, and the bed being soft and comfortable, Mr Quilp determined to use it, both as a sleeping place by night and as a kind of Divan by day. (The Old Curiosity Shop by Charles Dickens)*

divorcement NOUN separation ❑ *By all pains which want and* divorcement hath (*On His Mistress* by John Donne)

dog in the manger, PHRASE this phrase describes someone who prevents you from enjoying something that they themselves have no need for ❑ *You are a dog in the manger, Cathy, and desire no one to be loved but yourself* (*Wuthering Heights* by Emily Brontë)

dolorifuge NOUN dolorifuge is a word which Thomas Hardy invented. It means pain-killer or comfort ❑ *as a species of dolorifuge* (*Tess of the D'Urbervilles* by Thomas Hardy)

dome NOUN building ❑ *that river and that mouldering dome* (*The Prelude* by William Wordsworth)

domestic PHRASE here domestic means a person's management of the house ❑ *to give some account of my domestic* (*Gulliver's Travels* by Jonathan Swift)

dunce NOUN a dunce is another word for idiot ❑ *Do you take me for a dunce? Go on?* (*Alice's Adventures in Wonderland* by Lewis Carroll)

Ecod EXCLAM a slang exclamation meaning 'oh God!' ❑ *"Ecod," replied Wemmick, shaking his head, "that's not my trade."* (*Great Expectations* by Charles Dickens)

egg-hot NOUN an egg-hot (see also 'flip' and 'negus') was a hot drink made from beer and eggs, sweetened with nutmeg ❑ *She fainted when she saw me return, and made a little jug of egg-hot afterwards to console us while we talked it over.* (*David Copperfield* by Charles Dickens)

encores NOUN an encore is a short extra performance at the end of a longer one, which the entertainer gives because the audience has enthusiastically asked for it ❑ *we want a little something to answer encores with, anyway* (*The Adventures of Huckleberry Finn* by Mark Twain)

equipage NOUN an elegant and impressive carriage ❑ *and besides, the equipage did not answer to any of*

their neighbours (*Pride and Prejudice* by Jane Austen)

exordium NOUN an exordium is the opening part of a speech ❑ *"Now, Handel," as if it were the grave beginning of a portentous business exordium, he had suddenly given up that tone* (*Great Expectations* by Charles Dickens)

expect VERB here expect means to wait for ❑ *to expect his farther commands* (*Gulliver's Travels* by Jonathan Swift)

familiars NOUN familiars means spirits or devils who come to someone when they are called ❑ *I'll turn all the lice about here into familiars* (*Doctor Faustus 1.4* by Christopher Marlowe)

fantods NOUN a fantod is a person who fidgets or can't stop moving nervously ❑ *It most give me the fantods* (*The Adventures of Huckleberry Finn* by Mark Twain)

farthing NOUN a farthing is an old unit of British currency which was worth a quarter of a penny ❑ *Not a farthing less. A great many back-payments are included in it, I assure you.* (*A Christmas Carol* by Charles Dickens)

farthingale NOUN a hoop worn under a skirt to extend it ❑ *A bell with an old voice – which I dare say in its time had often said to the house, Here is the green farthingale* (*Great Expectations* by Charles Dickens)

favours NOUN here favours is an old word which means ribbons ❑ *A group of humble mourners entered the gate: wearing white favours* (*Oliver Twist* by Charles Dickens)

feigned VERB pretend or pretending ❑ *not my feigned page* (*On His Mistress* by John Donne)

fence ■ NOUN a fence is someone who receives and sells stolen goods ❑ *What are you up to? Ill-treating the boys, you covetous, avaricious, in-sa-ti-a-ble old fence?* (*Oliver Twist* by

Charles Dickens) ■ NOUN defence or protection ❑ *but honesty hath no fence against superior cunning* (*Gulliver's Travels* by Jonathan Swift)

fess ADJ fess is an old word which means pleased or proud ❑ *You'll be fess enough, my poppet* (*Tess of the D'Urbervilles* by Thomas Hardy)

fettered ADJ fettered means bound in chains or chained ❑ *"You are fettered," said Scrooge, trembling. "Tell me why?"* (*A Christmas Carol* by Charles Dickens)

fidges VERB fidges means fidgets, which is to keep moving your hands slightly because you are nervous or excited ❑ *Look, Jim, how my fingers fidges* (*Treasure Island* by Robert Louis Stevenson)

finger-post NOUN a finger-post is a sign-post showing the direction to different places ❑ *"The gallows," continued Fagin, "the gallows, my dear, is an ugly finger-post, which points out a very short and sharp turning that has stopped many a bold fellow's career on the broad highway."* (*Oliver Twist* by Charles Dickens)

fire-irons NOUN fire-irons are tools kept by the side of the fire to either cook with or look after the fire ❑ *the fire-irons came first* (*Alice's Adventures in Wonderland* by Lewis Carroll)

fire-plug NOUN a fire-plug is another word for a fire hydrant ❑ *The pony looked with great attention into a fire-plug, which was near him, and appeared to be quite absorbed in contemplating it* (*The Old Curiosity Shop* by Charles Dickens)

flank NOUN flank is the side of an animal ❑ *And all her silken flanks with garlands dressed* (*Ode on a Grecian Urn* by John Keats)

flip NOUN a flip is a drink made from warmed ale,sugar, spice and beaten egg ❑ *The events of the day, in combination with the twins, if not with the flip, had made Mrs. Micawber hysterical, and she shed tears as she replied* (*David Copperfield* by Charles Dickens)

flit VERB flit means to move quickly ❑ *and if he had meant to flit to Thrushcross Grange* (*Wuthering Heights* by Emily Brontë)

floorcloth NOUN a floorcloth was a hard-wearing piece of canvas used instead of carpet ❑ *This avenging phantom was ordered to be on duty at eight on Tuesday morning in the hall (it was two feet square, as charged for floorcloth)* (*Great Expectations* by Charles Dickens)

fly-driver NOUN a fly-driver is a carriage drawn by a single horse ❑ *The fly-drivers, among whom I inquired next, were equally jocose and equally disrespectful* (*David Copperfield* by Charles Dickens)

fob NOUN a small pocket in which a watch is kept ❑ *"Certain," replied the man, drawing a gold watch from his fob* (*Oliver Twist* by Charles Dickens)

folly NOUN folly means foolishness or stupidity ❑ *the folly of beginning a work* (*Robinson Crusoe* by Daniel Defoe)

fond ADJ fond means foolish ❑ *Fond worldling* (*Doctor Faustus 5.2* by Christopher Marlowe)

fondness NOUN silly or foolish affection ❑ *They have no fondness for their colts or foals* (*Gulliver's Travels* by Jonathan Swift)

for his fancy PHRASE for his fancy means for his liking or as he wanted ❑ *and as I did not obey quick enough for his fancy* (*Treasure Island* by Robert Louis Stevenson)

forlorn ADJ lost or very upset ❑ *you are from that day forlorn* (*Gulliver's Travels* by Jonathan Swift)

foster-sister NOUN a foster-sister was someone brought up by the same nurse or in the same household ❑ *I had been his foster-sister* (*Wuthering Heights* by Emily Brontë)

fox-fire NOUN fox-fire is a weak glow that is given off by decaying, rotten wood ❑ *what we must have was a lot of them rotten chunks* that's called fox-fire (*The Adventures of Huckleberry Finn* by Mark Twain)

frozen sea PHRASE the Arctic Ocean ❏ *into the frozen sea* (*Gulliver's Travels* by Jonathan Swift)

gainsay VERB to gainsay something is to say it isn't true or to deny it ❏ *"So she had," cried Scrooge. "You're right. I'll not gainsay it, Spirit. God forbid!"* (*A Christmas Carol* by Charles Dickens)

gaiters NOUN gaiters were leggings made of a cloth or piece of leather which covered the leg from the knee to the ankle ❏ *Mr Knightley was hard at work upon the lower buttons of his thick leather gaiters* (*Emma* by Jane Austen)

galluses NOUN galluses is an old spelling of gallows, and here means suspenders. Suspenders are straps worn over someone's shoulders and fastened to their trousers to prevent the trousers falling down ❏ *and home-knit galluses* (*The Adventures of Huckleberry Finn* by Mark Twain)

galoot NOUN a sailor but also a clumsy person ❏ *and maybe a galoot on it chopping* (*The Adventures of Huckleberry Finn* by Mark Twain)

gayest ADJ gayest means the most lively and bright or merry ❏ *Beth played her gayest march* (*Little Women* by Louisa May Alcott)

gem NOUN here gem means jewellery ❏ *the mountain shook off turf and flower, had only heath for raiment and crag for gem* (*Jane Eyre* by Charlotte Brontë)

giddy ADJ giddy means dizzy ❏ *and I wish you wouldn't keep appearing and vanishing so suddenly; you make one quite giddy.* (*Alice's Adventures in Wonderland* by Lewis Carroll)

gig NOUN a light two-wheeled carriage ❏ *when a gig drove up to the garden gate: out of which there jumped a fat gentleman* (*Oliver Twist* by Charles Dickens)

gladsome ADJ gladsome is an old word meaning glad or happy ❏ *Nobody ever stopped him in the street to say, with gladsome looks* (*A Christmas Carol* by Charles Dickens)

glen NOUN a glen is a small valley; the word is used commonly in Scotland ❏ *a beck which follows the bend of the glen* (*Wuthering Heights* by Emily Brontë)

gravelled VERB gravelled is an old term which means to baffle or defeat someone ❏ *Gravelled the pastors of the German Church* (*Doctor Faustus 1.1* by Christopher Marlowe)

grinder NOUN a grinder was a private tutor ❏ *but that when he had had the happiness of marrying Mrs Pocket very early in his life, he had impaired his prospects and taken up the calling of a Grinder* (*Great Expectations* by Charles Dickens)

gruel NOUN gruel is a thin, watery corn-meal or oatmeal soup ❏ *And the little saucepan of gruel (Scrooge had a cold in his head) upon the hob.* (*A Christmas Carol* by Charles Dickens)

guinea, half a NOUN a half guinea was ten shillings and sixpence ❏ *but lay out half a guinea at Ford's* (*Emma* by Jane Austen)

gull VERB gull is an old term which means to fool or deceive someone ❏ *Hush, I'll gull him supernaturally* (*Doctor Faustus 3.4* by Christopher Marlowe)

gunnel NOUN the gunnel, or gunwhale, is the upper edge of a boat's side ❏ *But he put his foot on the gunnel and rocked her* (*The Adventures of Huckleberry Finn* by Mark Twain)

gunwale NOUN the side of a ship ❏ *He dipped his hand in the water over the boat's gunwale* (*Great Expectations* by Charles Dickens)

Gytrash NOUN a Gytrash is an omen of misfortune to the superstitious, usually taking the form of a hound ❏ *I remembered certain of Bessie's tales, wherein figured a*

North-of-England spirit, called a 'Gytrash' (*Jane Eyre* by Charlotte Brontë)

hackney-cabriolet NOUN a two-wheeled carriage with four seats for hire and pulled by a horse ❑ *A hackney-cabriolet was in waiting; with the same vehemence which she had exhibited in addressing Oliver, the girl pulled him in with her, and drew the curtains close.* (*Oliver Twist* by Charles Dickens)

hackney-coach NOUN a four-wheeled horse-drawn vehicle for hire ❑ *The twilight was beginning to close in, when Mr. Brownlow alighted from a hackney-coach at his own door, and knocked softly.* (*Oliver Twist* by Charles Dickens)

haggler NOUN a haggler is someone who travels from place to place selling small goods and items ❑ *when I be plain Jack Durbeyfield, the haggler* (*Tess of the D'Urbervilles* by Thomas Hardy)

halter NOUN a halter is a rope or strap used to lead an animal or to tie it up ❑ *I had of course long been used to a halter and a headstall* (*Black Beauty* by Anna Sewell)

hamlet NOUN a hamlet is a small village or a group of houses in the countryside ❑ *down from the hamlet* (*Treasure Island* by Robert Louis Stevenson)

hand-barrow NOUN a hand-barrow is a device for carrying heavy objects. It is like a wheelbarrow except that it has handles, rather than wheels, for moving the barrow ❑ *his sea chest following behind him in a hand-barrow* (*Treasure Island* by Robert Louis Stevenson)

handspike NOUN a handspike was a stick which was used as a lever ❑ *a bit of stick like a handspike* (*Treasure Island* by Robert Louis Stevenson)

haply ADV haply means by chance or perhaps ❑ *And haply the Queen-Moon is on her throne* (*Ode on a Nightingale* by John Keats)

harem NOUN the harem was the part of the house where the women lived ❑ *mostly they hang round the harem* (*The Adventures of Huckleberry Finn* by Mark Twain)

hautboys NOUN hautboys are oboes ❑ *sausages and puddings resembling flutes and hautboys* (*Gulliver's Travels* by Jonathan Swift)

hawker NOUN a hawker is someone who sells goods to people as he travels rather than from a fixed place like a shop ❑ *to buy some stockings from a hawker* (*Treasure Island* by Robert Louis Stevenson)

hawser NOUN a hawser is a rope used to tie up or tow a ship or boat ❑ *Again among the tiers of shipping, in and out, avoiding rusty chain-cables, frayed hempen hawsers* (*Great Expectations* by Charles Dickens)

headstall NOUN the headstall is the part of the bridle or halter that goes around a horse's head ❑ *I had of course long been used to a halter and a headstall* (*Black Beauty* by Anna Sewell)

hearken VERB hearken means to listen ❑ *though we sometimes stopped to lay hold of each other and hearken* (*Treasure Island* by Robert Louis Stevenson)

heartless ADJ here heartless means without heart or dejected ❑ *I am not heartless* (*The Prelude* by William Wordsworth)

hebdomadal ADJ hebdomadal means weekly ❑ *It was the hebdomadal treat to which we all looked forward from Sabbath to Sabbath* (*Jane Eyre* by Charlotte Brontë)

highwaymen NOUN highwaymen were people who stopped travellers and robbed them ❑ *We are highwaymen* (*The Adventures of Huckleberry Finn* by Mark Twain)

hinds NOUN hinds means farm hands, or people who work on a farm ❑ *He called his hinds about him* (*Gulliver's Travels* by Jonathan Swift)

histrionic ADJ if you refer to someone's behaviour as histrionic, you are being critical of it because it is dramatic and exaggerated ❑ *But the histrionic muse is the darling* (*The Adventures of Huckleberry Finn* by Mark Twain)

hogs NOUN hogs is another word for pigs ❑ *Tom called the hogs 'ingots'* (*The Adventures of Huckleberry Finn* by Mark Twain)

horrors NOUN the horrors are a fit, called delirium tremens, which is caused by drinking too much alcohol ❑ *I'll have the horrors* (*Treasure Island* by Robert Louis Stevenson)

huffy ADJ huffy means to be obviously annoyed or offended about something ❑ *They will feel that more than angry speeches or huffy actions* (*Little Women* by Louisa May Alcott)

hulks NOUN hulks were prison-ships ❑ *The miserable companion of thieves and ruffians, the fallen outcast of low haunts, the associate of the scourings of the jails and hulks* (*Oliver Twist* by Charles Dickens)

humbug NOUN humbug means nonsense or rubbish ❑ *"Bah," said Scrooge. "Humbug!"* (*A Christmas Carol* by Charles Dickens)

humours NOUN it was believed that there were four fluids in the body called humours which decided the temperament of a person depending on how much of each fluid was present ❑ *other peccant humours* (*Gulliver's Travels* by Jonathan Swift)

husbandry NOUN husbandry is farming animals ❑ *bad husbandry were plentifully anointing their wheels* (*Silas Marner* by George Eliot)

huswife NOUN a huswife was a small sewing kit ❑ *but I had put my huswife on it* (*Emma* by Jane Austen)

ideal ADJ ideal in this context means imaginary ❑ *I discovered the yell was not ideal* (*Wuthering Heights* by Emily Brontë)

If our two PHRASE if both our ❑ *If our two loves be one* (*The Good-Morrow* by John Donne)

ignis-fatuus NOUN ignis-fatuus is the light given out by burning marsh gases, which lead careless travellers into danger ❑ *it is madness in all women to let a secret love kindle within them, which, if unreturned and unknown, must devour the life that feeds it; and, if discovered and responded to, must lead ignis-fatuus-like, into miry wilds whence there is no extrication.* (*Jane Eyre* by Charlotte Brontë)

imaginations NOUN here imaginations means schemes or plans ❑ *soon drove out those imaginations* (*Gulliver's Travels* by Jonathan Swift)

impressible ADJ impressible means open or impressionable ❑ *for Marner had one of those impressible, self-doubting natures* (*Silas Marner* by George Eliot)

in good intelligence PHRASE friendly with each other ❑ *that these two persons were in good intelligence with each other* (*Gulliver's Travels* by Jonathan Swift)

inanity NOUN inanity is sillyness or dull stupidity ❑ *Do we not wile away moments of inanity* (*Silas Marner* by George Eliot)

incivility NOUN incivility means rudeness or impoliteness ❑ *if it's only for a piece of incivility like to-night's* (*Treasure Island* by Robert Louis Stevenson)

indigenae NOUN indigenae means natives or people from that area ❑ *an exotic that the surly indigenae will not recognise for kin* (*Wuthering Heights* by Emily Brontë)

indocible ADJ unteachable ❑ *so they were the most restive and indocible* (*Gulliver's Travels* by Jonathan Swift)

ingenuity NOUN inventiveness ❑ *entreated me to give him something as an encouragement to ingenuity*

(*Gulliver's Travels* by Jonathan Swift)

ingots NOUN an ingot is a lump of a valuable metal like gold, usually shaped like a brick ❏ *Tom called the hogs 'ingots'* (*The Adventures of Huckleberry Finn* by Mark Twain)

inkstand NOUN an inkstand is a pot which was put on a desk to contain either ink or pencils and pens ❏ *throwing an inkstand at the Lizard as she spoke* (*Alice's Adventures in Wonderland* by Lewis Carroll)

inordinate ADJ without order. Today inordinate means 'excessive'. ❏ *Though yet untutored and inordinate* (*The Prelude* by William Wordsworth)

intellectuals NOUN here intellectuals means the minds (of the workmen) ❏ *those instructions they give being too refined for the intellectuals of their workmen* (*Gulliver's Travels* by Jonathan Swift)

interview NOUN meeting ❏ *By our first strange and fatal interview* (*On His Mistress* by John Donne)

jacks NOUN jacks are rods for turning a spit over a fire ❏ It was a small bit of pork suspended from the kettle hanger by a string passed through a large door key, in a *way known to primitive housekeepers unpossessed of jacks* (*Silas Marner* by George Eliot)

jews-harp NOUN a jews-harp is a small, metal, musical instrument that is played by the mouth ❏ *A jews-harp's plenty good enough for a rat* (*The Adventures of Huckleberry Finn* by Mark Twain)

jorum NOUN a large bowl ❏ *while Miss Skiffins brewed such a jorum of tea, that the pig in the back premises became strongly excited* (*Great Expectations* by Charles Dickens)

jostled VERB jostled means bumped or pushed by someone or some people ❏ *being jostled himself into the kennel* (*Gulliver's Travels* by Jonathan Swift)

keepsake NOUN a keepsake is a gift which reminds someone of an event or of the person who gave it to them. ❏ *books and ornaments they had in their boudoirs at home: keepsakes that different relations had presented to them* (*Jane Eyre* by Charlotte Brontë)

kenned VERB kenned means knew ❏ *though little kenned the lamplighter that he had any company but Christmas!* (*A Christmas Carol* by Charles Dickens)

kennel NOUN kennel means gutter, which is the edge of a road next to the pavement, where rain water collects and flows away ❏ *being jostled himself into the kennel* (*Gulliver's Travels* by Jonathan Swift)

knock-knee ADJ knock-knee means slanted, at an angle. ❏ *LOT 1 was marked in whitewashed knock-knee letters on the brewhouse* (*Great Expectations* by Charles Dickens)

ladylike ADJ to be ladylike is to behave in a polite, dignified and graceful way ❏ *No, winking isn't ladylike* (*Little Women* by Louisa May Alcott)

lapse NOUN flow ❏ *Stealing with silent lapse to join the brook* (*The Prelude* by William Wordsworth)

larry NOUN larry is an old word which means commotion or noisy celebration ❏ *That was all a part of the larry!* (*Tess of the D'Urbervilles* by Thomas Hardy)

laths NOUN laths are strips of wood ❏ *The panels shrunk, the windows cracked; fragments of plaster fell out of the ceiling, and the naked laths were shown instead* (*A Christmas Carol* by Charles Dickens)

leer NOUN a leer is an unpleasant smile ❏ *with a kind of leer* (*Treasure Island* by Robert Louis Stevenson)

lenitives NOUN these are different kinds of drugs or medicines: lenitives and palliatives were pain relievers; aperitives were laxatives;

abstersives caused vomiting; corrosives destroyed human tissue; restringents caused constipation; cephalalgics stopped headaches; icterics were used as medicine for jaundice; apophlegmatics were cough medicine, and acoustics were cures for the loss of hearing ❑ *lenitives, aperitives, abstersives, corrosives, restringents, palliatives, laxatives, cephalalgics, icterics, apophlegmatics, acoustics* (*Gulliver's Travels* by Jonathan Swift)

lest CONJ in case. If you do something lest something (usually) unpleasant happens you do it to try to prevent it happening ❑ *She went in without knocking, and hurried upstairs, in great fear lest she should meet the real Mary Ann* (*Alice's Adventures in Wonderland* by Lewis Carroll)

levee NOUN a levee is an old term for a meeting held in the morning, shortly after the person holding the meeting has got out of bed ❑ *I used to attend the King's levee once or twice a week* (*Gulliver's Travels* by Jonathan Swift)

life-preserver NOUN a club which had lead inside it to make it heavier and therefore more dangerous ❑ *and with no more suspicious articles displayed to view than two or three heavy bludgeons which stood in a corner, and a 'life-preserver' that hung over the chimney-piece.* (*Oliver Twist* by Charles Dickens)

lighterman NOUN a lighterman is another word for sailor ❑ *in and out, hammers going in ship-builders' yards, saws going at timber, clashing engines going at things unknown, pumps going in leaky ships, capstans going, ships going out to sea, and unintelligible sea creatures roaring curses over the bulwarks at respondent lightermen* (*Great Expectations* by Charles Dickens)

livery NOUN servants often wore a uniform known as a livery ❑ *suddenly a footman in livery came running out of the wood* (*Alice's Adventures in Wonderland* by Lewis Carroll)

livid ADJ livid means pale or ash coloured. Livid also means very angry ❑ *a dirty, livid white* (*Treasure Island* by Robert Louis Stevenson)

lottery-tickets NOUN a popular card game ❑ *and Mrs. Philips protested that they would have a nice comfortable noisy game of lottery tickets* (*Pride and Prejudice* by Jane Austen)

lower and upper world PHRASE the earth and the heavens are the lower and upper worlds ❑ *the changes in the lower and upper world* (*Gulliver's Travels* by Jonathan Swift)

lustres NOUN lustres are chandeliers. A chandelier is a large, decorative frame which holds light bulbs or candles and hangs from the ceiling ❑ *the lustres, lights, the carving and the guilding* (*The Prelude* by William Wordsworth)

lynched VERB killed without a criminal trial by a crowd of people ❑ *He'll never know how nigh he come to getting lynched* (*The Adventures of Huckleberry Finn* by Mark Twain)

malingering VERB if someone is malingering they are pretending to be ill to avoid working ❑ *And you stand there malingering* (*Treasure Island* by Robert Louis Stevenson)

managing PHRASE treating with consideration ❑ *to think the honour of my own kind not worth managing* (*Gulliver's Travels* by Jonathan Swift)

manhood PHRASE manhood means human nature ❑ *concerning the nature of manhood* (*Gulliver's Travels* by Jonathan Swift)

man-trap NOUN a man-trap is a set of steel jaws that snap shut when trodden on and trap a person's leg ❑ *"Don't go to him," I called out of the window, "he's an assassin! A* man-trap!" (*Oliver Twist* by Charles Dickens)

maps NOUN charts of the night sky ❑ *Let maps to others, worlds on worlds have shown* (*The Good-Morrow* by John Donne)

mark VERB look at or notice ❑ *Mark but this flea, and mark in this* (*The Flea* by John Donne)

maroons NOUN A maroon is someone who has been left in a place which it is difficult for them to escape from, like a small island ❑ *if schooners, islands, and maroons* (*Treasure Island* by Robert Louis Stevenson)

mast NOUN here mast means the fruit of forest trees ❑ *a quantity of acorns, dates, chestnuts, and other mast* (*Gulliver's Travels* by Jonathan Swift)

mate VERB defeat ❑ *Where Mars did mate the warlike Carthigens* (*Doctor Faustus Chorus* by Christopher Marlowe)

mealy ADJ Mealy when used to describe a face meant palid, pale or colourless ❑ *I only know two sorts of boys. Mealy boys, and beef-faced boys* (*Oliver Twist* by Charles Dickens)

middling ADJ fairly or moderately ❑ *she worked me middling hard for about an hour* (*The Adventures of Huckleberry Finn* by Mark Twain)

mill NOUN a mill, or treadmill, was a device for hard labour or punishment in prison ❑ *Was you never on the mill?* (*Oliver Twist* by Charles Dickens)

milliner's shop NOUN a milliner's sold fabrics, clothing, lace and accessories; as time went on they specialized more and more in hats ❑ *to pay their duty to their aunt and to a milliner's shop just over the way* (*Pride and Prejudice* by Jane Austen)

minching un' munching PHRASE how people in the north of England used to describe the way people from the south speak ❑ *Minching*

un' munching! (*Wuthering Heights* by Emily Brontë)

mine NOUN gold ❑ *Whether both th'Indias of spice and mine* (*The Sun Rising* by John Donne)

mire NOUN mud ❑ *Tis my fate to be always ground into the mire under the iron heel of oppression* (*The Adventures of Huckleberry Finn* by Mark Twain)

miscellany NOUN a miscellany is a collection of many different kinds of things ❑ *under that, the miscellany began* (*Treasure Island* by Robert Louis Stevenson)

mistarshers NOUN mistarshers means moustache, which is the hair that grows on a man's upper lip ❑ *when he put his hand up to his mistarshers* (*Tess of the D'Urbervilles* by Thomas Hardy)

morrow NOUN here good-morrow means tomorrow and a new and better life ❑ *And now good-morrow to our waking souls* (*The Good-Morrow* by John Donne)

mortification NOUN mortification is an old word for gangrene which is when part of the body decays or 'dies' because of disease ❑ *Yes, it was a mortification – that was it* (*The Adventures of Huckleberry Finn* by Mark Twain)

mought PARTICIPLE mought is an old spelling of might ❑ *what you mought call me? You mought call me captain* (*Treasure Island* by Robert Louis Stevenson)

move VERB move me not means do not make me angry ❑ *Move me not, Faustus* (*Doctor Faustus 2.1* by Christopher Marlowe)

muffin-cap NOUN a muffin cap is a flat cap made from wool ❑ *the old one, remained stationary in the muffin-cap and leathers* (*Oliver Twist* by Charles Dickens)

mulatter NOUN a mulatter was another word for mulatto, which is a person with parents who are from different races ❑ *a mulatter, most as white as* a white man (*The Adventures of Huckleberry Finn* by Mark Twain)

mummery NOUN mummery is an old word that meant meaningless (or pretentious) ceremony ❑ *When they were all gone, and when Trabb and his men – but not his boy: I looked for him – had crammed their mummery into bags, and were gone too, the house felt wholesomer.* (*Great Expectations* by Charles Dickens)

nap NOUN the nap is the woolly surface on a new item of clothing. Here the surface has been worn away so it looks bare ❑ *like an old hat with the nap rubbed off* (*The Adventures of Huckleberry Finn* by Mark Twain)

natural ■ NOUN a natural is a person born with learning difficulties ❑ *though he had been left to his particular care by their deceased father, who thought him almost a natural.* (*David Copperfield* by Charles Dickens) ■ ADJ natural meant illegitimate ❑ *Harriet Smith was the natural daughter of some- body* (*Emma* by Jane Austen)

navigator NOUN a navigator was originally someone employed to dig canals. It is the origin of the word 'navvy' meaning a labourer ❑ *She ascertained from me in a few words what it was all about, comforted Dora, and gradually convinced her that I was not a labourer – from my manner of stating the case I believe Dora concluded that I was a navi- gator, and went balancing myself up and down a plank all day with a wheelbarrow – and so brought us together in peace.* (*David Copperfield* by Charles Dickens)

necromancy NOUN necromancy means a kind of magic where the magician speaks to spirits or ghosts to find out what will happen in the future ❑ *He surfeits upon cursed necro- mancy* (*Doctor Faustus chorus* by Christopher Marlowe)

negus NOUN a negus is a hot drink made from sweetened wine and water ❑ *He sat placidly perusing the newspaper, with his little head on one side, and a glass of warm sherry negus at his elbow.* (*David Copperfield* by Charles Dickens)

nice ADJ discriminating. Able to make good judgements or choices ❑ *consequently a claim to be nice* (*Emma* by Jane Austen)

nigh ADV nigh means near ❑ *He'll never know how nigh he come to getting lynched* (*The Adventures of Huckleberry Finn* by Mark Twain)

nimbleness NOUN nimbleness means being able to move very quickly or skillfully ❑ *and with incredible accuracy and nimbleness* (*Treasure Island* by Robert Louis Stevenson)

noggin NOUN a noggin is a small mug or a wooden cup ❑ *you'll bring me one noggin of rum* (*Treasure Island* by Robert Louis Stevenson)

none ADJ neither ❑ *none can die* (*The Good-Morrow* by John Donne)

notices NOUN observations ❑ *Arch are his notices* (*The Prelude* by William Wordsworth)

occiput NOUN occiput means the back of the head ❑ *saw off the occiput of each couple* (*Gulliver's Travels* by Jonathan Swift)

officiously ADJ kindly ❑ *the governess who attended Glumdalclitch very officiously lifted me up* (*Gulliver's Travels* by Jonathan Swift)

old salt PHRASE old salt is a slang term for an experienced sailor ❑ *a 'true sea-dog', and a 'real old salt'* (*Treasure Island* by Robert Louis Stevenson)

or ere PHRASE before ❑ *or ere the Hall was built* (*The Prelude* by William Wordsworth)

ostler NOUN one who looks after horses at an inn ❑ *The bill paid, and the waiter remembered, and the ostler not forgotten, and the chambermaid taken into consideration* (*Great Expectations* by Charles Dickens)

ostry NOUN an ostry is an old word for a pub or hotel ❑ *lest I send you into the ostry with a vengeance* (*Doctor Faustus* 2.2 by Christopher Marlowe)

outrunning the constable PHRASE outrunning the constable meant spending more than you earn ❑ *but I shall by this means be able to check your bills and to pull you up if I find you outrunning the constable.* (*Great Expectations* by Charles Dickens)

over ADJ across ❑ *It is in length six yards, and in the thickest part at least three yards over* (*Gulliver's Travels* by Jonathan Swift)

over the broomstick PHRASE this is a phrase meaning 'getting married without a formal ceremony' ❑ *They both led tramping lives, and this woman in Gerrard-street here, had been married very young, over the broomstick (as we say), to a tramping man, and was a perfect fury in point of jealousy.* (*Great Expectations* by Charles Dickens)

own VERB own means to admit or to acknowledge ❑ *It's my old girl that advises. She has the head. But I never own to it before her. Discipline must be maintained* (*Bleak House* by Charles Dickens)

page NOUN here page means a boy employed to run errands ❑ *not my feigned page* (*On His Mistress* by John Donne)

paid pretty dear PHRASE paid pretty dear means paid a high price or suffered quite a lot ❑ *I paid pretty dear for my monthly fourpenny piece* (*Treasure Island* by Robert Louis Stevenson)

pannikins NOUN pannikins were small tin cups ❑ *of lifting light glasses and cups to his lips, as if they were clumsy pannikins* (*Great Expectations* by Charles Dickens)

pards NOUN pards are leopards ❑ *Not charioted by Bacchus and his pards* (*Ode on a Nightingale* by John Keats)

parlour boarder NOUN a pupil who lived with the family ❑ *and somebody had lately raised her from the condition of scholar to parlour boarder* (*Emma* by Jane Austen)

particular, a London PHRASE London in Victorian times and up to the 1950s was famous for having very dense fog – which was a combination of real fog and the smog of pollution from factories ❑ *This is a London particular . . . A fog, miss'* (*Bleak House* by Charles Dickens)

patten NOUN pattens were wooden soles which were fixed to shoes by straps to protect the shoes in wet weather ❑ *carrying a basket like the Great Seal of England in plaited straw, a pair of pattens, a spare shawl, and an umbrella, though it was a fine bright day* (*Great Expectations* by Charles Dickens)

paviour NOUN a paviour was a labourer who worked on the street pavement ❑ *the paviour his pickaxe* (*Oliver Twist* by Charles Dickens)

peccant ADJ peccant means unhealthy ❑ *other peccant humours* (*Gulliver's Travels* by Jonathan Swift)

penetralium NOUN penetralium is a word used to describe the inner rooms of the house ❑ *and I had no desire to aggravate his impatience previous to inspecting the penetralium* (*Wuthering Heights* by Emily Brontë)

pensive ADV pensive means deep in thought or thinking seriously about something ❑ *and she was leaning pensive on a tomb-stone on her right elbow* (*The Adventures of Huckleberry Finn* by Mark Twain)

penury NOUN penury is the state of being extremely poor ❑ *Distress, if not penury, loomed in the distance* (*Tess of the D'Urbervilles* by Thomas Hardy)

perspective NOUN telescope ❑ *a pocket perspective* (*Gulliver's Travels* by Jonathan Swift)

phaeton NOUN a phaeton was an open carriage for four people ❑ *often* condescends to drive by my humble abode in her little phaeton and ponies (*Pride and Prejudice* by Jane Austen)

phantasm NOUN a phantasm is an illusion, something that is not real. It is sometimes used to mean ghost ❑ *Experience had bred no fancies in him that could raise the phantasm of appetite* (*Silas Marner* by George Eliot)

physic NOUN here physic means medicine ❑ *there I studied physic two years and seven months* (*Gulliver's Travels* by Jonathan Swift)

pinioned VERB to pinion is to hold both arms so that a person cannot move them ❑ *But the relentless Ghost pinioned him in both his arms, and forced him to observe what happened next.* (*A Christmas Carol* by Charles Dickens)

piquet NOUN piquet was a popular card game in the C18th ❑ *Mr Hurst and Mr Bingley were at piquet* (*Pride and Prejudice* by Jane Austen)

plaister NOUN a plaister is a piece of cloth on which an apothecary (or pharmacist) would spread ointment. The cloth is then applied to wounds or bruises to treat them ❑ *Then, she gave the knife a final smart wipe on the edge of the plaister, and then sawed a very thick round off the loaf: which she finally, before separating from the loaf, hewed into two halves, of which Joe got one, and I the other.* (*Great Expectations* by Charles Dickens)

plantations NOUN here plantations means colonies, which are countries controlled by a more powerful country ❑ *besides our plantations in America* (*Gulliver's Travels* by Jonathan Swift)

plastic ADV here plastic is an old term meaning shaping or a power that was forming ❑ *A plastic power abode with me* (*The Prelude* by William Wordsworth)

players NOUN actors ❑ *of players which*

upon the world's stage be (*On His Mistress* by John Donne)

plump ADV all at once, suddenly ❑ *But it took a bit of time to get it well round, the change come so uncommon plump, didn't it?* (*Great Expectations* by Charles Dickens)

plundered VERB to plunder is to rob or steal from ❑ *These crosses stand for the names of ships or towns that they sank or plundered* (*Treasure Island* by Robert Louis Stevenson)

pommel ■ VERB to pommel someone is to hit them repeatedly with your fists ❑ *hug him round the neck, pommel his back, and kick his legs in irrepressible affection!* (*A Christmas Carol* by Charles Dickens) ■ NOUN a pommel is the part of a saddle that rises up at the front ❑ *He had his gun across his pommel* (*The Adventures of Huckleberry Finn* by Mark Twain)

poor's rates NOUN poor's rates were property taxes which were used to support the poor ❑ *"Oh!" replied the undertaker; "why, you know, Mr. Bumble, I pay a good deal towards the poor's rates."* (*Oliver Twist* by Charles Dickens)

popular ADJ popular means ruled by the people, or Republican, rather than ruled by a monarch ❑ *With those of Greece compared and popular Rome* (*The Prelude* by William Wordsworth)

porringer NOUN a porringer is a small bowl ❑ *Of this festive composition each boy had one porringer, and no more* (*Oliver Twist* by Charles Dickens)

postboy NOUN a postboy was the driver of a horse-drawn carriage ❑ *He spoke to a postboy who was dozing under the gateway* (*Oliver Twist* by Charles Dickens)

post-chaise NOUN a fast carriage for two or four passengers ❑ *Looking round, he saw that it was a post-chaise, driven at great speed* (*Oliver Twist* by Charles Dickens)

postern NOUN a small gate usually at the back of a building ❑ *The little servant happening to be entering the fortress with two hot rolls, I passed through the postern and crossed the drawbridge, in her company* (*Great Expectations* by Charles Dickens)

pottle NOUN a pottle was a small basket ❑ *He had a paper-bag under each arm and a pottle of strawberries in one hand . . .* (*Great Expectations* by Charles Dickens)

pounce NOUN pounce is a fine powder used to prevent ink spreading on untreated paper ❑ *in that grim atmosphere of pounce and parchment, red-tape, dusty wafers, ink-jars, brief and draft paper, law reports, writs, declarations, and bills of costs* (*David Copperfield* by Charles Dickens)

pox NOUN pox means sexually transmitted diseases like syphilis ❑ *how the pox in all its consequences and denominations* (*Gulliver's Travels* by Jonathan Swift)

prelibation NOUN prelibation means a foretaste of or an example of something to come ❑ *A prelibation to the mower's scythe* (*The Prelude* by William Wordsworth)

prentice NOUN an apprentice ❑ *and Joe, sitting on an old gun, had told me that when I was 'prentice to him regularly bound, we would have such Larks there!* (*Great Expectations* by Charles Dickens)

presently ADV immediately ❑ *I presently knew what they meant* (*Gulliver's Travels* by Jonathan Swift)

pumpion NOUN pumpkin ❑ *for it was almost as large as a small pumpion* (*Gulliver's Travels* by Jonathan Swift)

punctual ADJ kept in one place ❑ *was not a punctual presence, but a spirit* (*The Prelude* by William Wordsworth)

quadrille ■ NOUN a quadrille is a dance invented in France which is usually performed by four couples ❑ *However, Mr Swiveller had Miss Sophy's hand for the first quadrille (country-dances being low, were utterly proscribed)* (*The Old Curiosity Shop* by Charles Dickens) ■ NOUN quadrille was a card game for four people ❑ *to make up her pool of quadrille in the evening* (*Pride and Prejudice* by Jane Austen)

quality NOUN gentry or upper-class people ❑ *if you are with the quality* (*The Adventures of Huckleberry Finn* by Mark Twain)

quick parts PHRASE quick-witted ❑ *Mr Bennet was so odd a mixture of quick parts* (*Pride and Prejudice* by Jane Austen)

quid NOUN a quid is something chewed or kept in the mouth, like a piece of tobacco ❑ *rolling his quid* (*Treasure Island* by Robert Louis Stevenson)

quit VERB quit means to avenge or to make even ❑ *But Faustus's death shall quit my infamy* (*Doctor Faustus 4.3* by Christopher Marlowe)

rags NOUN divisions ❑ *Nor hours, days, months, which are the rags of time* (*The Sun Rising* by John Donne)

raiment NOUN raiment means clothing ❑ *the mountain shook off turf and flower, had only heath for raiment and crag for gem* (*Jane Eyre* by Charlotte Brontë)

rain cats and dogs PHRASE an expression meaning rain heavily. The origin of the expression is unclear ❑ *But it'll perhaps rain cats and dogs to-morrow* (*Silas Marner* by George Eliot)

raised Cain PHRASE raised Cain means caused a lot of trouble. Cain is a character in the Bible who killed his brother Abel ❑ *and every time he got drunk he raised Cain around town* (*The Adventures of Huckleberry Finn* by Mark Twain)

rambling ADJ rambling means confused and not very clear ❑ *my* *head began to be filled very early with rambling thoughts* (*Robinson Crusoe* by Daniel Defoe)

raree-show NOUN a raree-show is an old term for a peep-show or a fairground entertainment ❏ *A raree-show is here, with children gathered round* (*The Prelude* by William Wordsworth)

recusants NOUN people who resisted authority ❏ *hardy recusants* (*The Prelude* by William Wordsworth)

redounding VERB eddying. An eddy is a movement in water or air which goes round and round instead of flowing in one direction ❏ *mists and steam-like fogs redounding everywhere* (*The Prelude* by William Wordsworth)

redundant ADJ here redundant means overflowing but Wordsworth also uses it to mean excessively large or too big ❏ *A tempest, a redundant energy* (*The Prelude* by William Wordsworth)

reflex NOUN reflex is a shortened version of reflexion, which is an alternative spelling of reflection ❏ *To cut across the reflex of a star* (*The Prelude* by William Wordsworth)

Reformatory NOUN a prison for young offenders/criminals ❏ *Even when I was taken to have a new suit of clothes, the tailor had orders to make them like a kind of Reformatory, and on no account to let me have the free use of my limbs.* (*Great Expectations* by Charles Dickens)

remorse NOUN pity or compassion ❏ *by that remorse* (*On His Mistress* by John Donne)

render VERB in this context render means give. ❏ *and Sarah could render no reason that would be sanctioned by the feeling of the community.* (*Silas Marner* by George Eliot)

repeater NOUN a repeater was a watch that chimed the last hour when a button was pressed – as a result it was useful in the dark ❏ *And his watch is a gold repeater, and worth a hundred pound if it's worth a penny.* (*Great Expectations* by Charles Dickens)

repugnance NOUN repugnance means a strong dislike of something or someone ❏ *overcoming a strong repugnance* (*Treasure Island* by Robert Louis Stevenson)

reverence NOUN reverence means bow. When you bow to someone, you briefly bend your body towards them as a formal way of showing them respect ❏ *made my reverence* (*Gulliver's Travels* by Jonathan Swift)

reverie NOUN a reverie is a day dream ❏ *I can guess the subject of your reverie* (*Pride and Prejudice* by Jane Austen)

revival NOUN a religious meeting held in public ❏ *well I'd ben a-running' a little temperance revival thar' bout a week* (*The Adventures of Huckleberry Finn* by Mark Twain)

revolt VERB revolt means turn back or stop your present course of action and go back to what you were doing before ❏ *Revolt, or I'll in piecemeal tear thy flesh* (*Doctor Faustus 5.1* by Christopher Marlowe)

rheumatics/rheumatism NOUN rheumatics [rheumatism] is an illness that makes your joints or muscles stiff and painful ❏ *a new cure for the rheumatics* (*Treasure Island* by Robert Louis Stevenson)

riddance NOUN riddance is usually used in the form good riddance which you say when you are pleased that something has gone or been left behind ❏ *I'd better go into the house, and die and be a riddance* (*David Copperfield* by Charles Dickens)

rimy ADJ rimy is an ADJECTIVE which means covered in ice or frost ❏ *It was a rimy morning, and very damp* (*Great Expectations* by Charles Dickens)

riper ADJ riper means more mature or older ❏ *At riper years to Wittenberg he went* (*Doctor Faustus* chorus by Christopher Marlowe)

rubber NOUN a set of games in whist or backgammon ❏ *her father was sure of his rubber* (*Emma* by Jane Austen)

ruffian NOUN a ruffian is a person who behaves violently ❏ *and when the ruffian had told him* (*Treasure Island* by Robert Louis Stevenson)

sadness NOUN sadness is an old term meaning seriousness ❏ *But I prithee tell me, in good sadness* (*Doctor Faustus* 2.2 by Christopher Marlowe)

sailed before the mast PHRASE this phrase meant someone who did not look like a sailor ❏ *he had none of the appearance of a man that sailed before the mast* (*Treasure Island* by Robert Louis Stevenson)

scabbard NOUN a scabbard is the covering for a sword or dagger ❏ *Girded round its middle was an antique scabbard; but no sword was in it, and the ancient sheath was eaten up with rust* (*A Christmas Carol* by Charles Dickens)

schooners NOUN A schooner is a fast, medium-sized sailing ship ❏ *if schooners, islands, and maroons* (*Treasure Island* by Robert Louis Stevenson)

science NOUN learning or knowledge ❏ *Even Science, too, at hand* (*The Prelude* by William Wordsworth)

scrouge VERB to scrouge means to squeeze or to crowd ❏ *to scrouge in and get a sight* (*The Adventures of Huckleberry Finn* by Mark Twain)

scrutore NOUN a scrutore, or escritoire, was a writing table ❏ *set me gently on my feet upon the scrutore* (*Gulliver's Travels* by Jonathan Swift)

scutcheon/escutcheon NOUN an escutcheon is a shield with a coat of arms, or the symbols of a family name, engraved on it ❏ *On the scutcheon we'll have a bend* (*The Adventures of Huckleberry Finn* by Mark Twain)

sea-dog PHRASE sea-dog is a slang term for an experienced sailor or pirate ❏ *a 'true sea-dog', and a 'real old salt,'* (*Treasure Island* by Robert Louis Stevenson)

see the lions PHRASE to see the lions was to go and see the sights of London. Originally the phrase referred to the menagerie in the Tower of London and later in Regent's Park ❏ *We will go and see the lions for an hour or two – it's something to have a fresh fellow like you to show them to, Copperfield* (*David Copperfield* by Charles Dickens)

self-conceit NOUN self-conceit is an old term which means having too high an opinion of oneself, or deceiving yourself ❏ *Till swollen with cunning, of a self-conceit* (*Doctor Faustus* chorus by Christopher Marlowe)

seneschal NOUN a steward ❏ *where a grey-headed seneschal sings a funny chorus with a funnier body of vassals* (*Oliver Twist* by Charles Dickens)

sensible ADJ if you were sensible of something you are aware or conscious of something ❏ *If my children are silly I must hope to be always sensible of it* (*Pride and Prejudice* by Jane Austen)

sessions NOUN court cases were heard at specific times of the year called sessions ❏ *He lay in prison very ill, during the whole interval between his committal for trial, and the coming round of the Sessions.* (*Great Expectations* by Charles Dickens)

shabby ADJ shabby places look old and in bad condition ❏ *a little bit of a shabby village named Pikesville* (*The Adventures of Huckleberry Finn* by Mark Twain)

shay-cart NOUN a shay-cart was a small cart drawn by one horse ❏ *"I were at the Bargemen t'other night, Pip;"*

whenever he subsided into affection, he called me Pip, and whenever he relapsed into politeness he called me Sir; "when there come up in his shay-cart Pumblechook." (Great Expectations by Charles Dickens)

shilling NOUN a shilling is an old unit of currency. There were twenty shillings in every British pound ❑ *"Ten shillings too much," said the gentleman in the white waistcoat. (Oliver Twist by Charles Dickens)*

shines NOUN tricks or games ❑ *well, it would make a cow laugh to see the shines that old idiot cut (The Adventures of Huckleberry Finn by Mark Twain)*

shirking VERB shirking means not doing what you are meant to be doing, or evading your duties ❑ *some of you shirking lubbers (Treasure Island by Robert Louis Stevenson)*

shiver my timbers PHRASE shiver my timbers is an expression which was used by sailors and pirates to express surprise ❑ *why, shiver my timbers, if I hadn't forgotten my score! (Treasure Island by Robert Louis Stevenson)*

shoe-roses NOUN shoe-roses were roses made from ribbons which were stuck on to shoes as decoration ❑ *the very shoe-roses for Netherfield were got by proxy (Pride and Prejudice by Jane Austen)*

singular ADJ singular means very great and remarkable or strange ❑ *"Singular dream," he says (The Adventures of Huckleberry Finn by Mark Twain)*

sire NOUN sire is an old word which means lord or master or elder ❑ *She also defied her sire (Little Women by Louisa May Alcott)*

sixpence NOUN a sixpence was half of a shilling ❑ *if she had only a shilling in the world, she would be very lilkely to give away sixpence of it (Emma by Jane Austen)*

slavey NOUN the word slavey was used when there was only one servant in

a house or boarding-house – so she had to perform all the duties of a larger staff ❑ *Two distinct knocks, sir, will produce the slavey at any time (The Old Curiosity Shop by Charles Dickens)*

slender ADJ weak ❑ *In slender accents of sweet verse (The Prelude by William Wordsworth)*

slop-shops NOUN slop-shops were shops where cheap ready-made clothes were sold. They mainly sold clothes to sailors ❑ *Accordingly, I took the jacket off, that I might learn to do without it; and carrying it under my arm, began a tour of inspection of the various slop-shops. (David Copperfield by Charles Dickens)*

sluggard NOUN a lazy person ❑ *"Stand up and repeat 'Tis the voice of the sluggard,'" said the Gryphon. (Alice's Adventures in Wonderland by Lewis Carroll)*

smallpox NOUN smallpox is a serious infectious disease ❑ *by telling the men we had smallpox aboard (The Adventures of Huckleberry Finn by Mark Twain)*

smalls NOUN smalls are short trousers ❑ *It is difficult for a large-headed, small-eyed youth, of lumbering make and heavy countenance, to look dignified under any circumstances; but it is more especially so, when superadded to these personal attractions are a red nose and yellow smalls (Oliver Twist by Charles Dickens)*

sneeze-box NOUN a box for snuff was called a sneeze-box because sniffing snuff makes the user sneeze ❑ *To think of Jack Dawkins — lummy Jack — the Dodger — the Artful Dodger — going abroad for a common twopenny-halfpenny sneeze-box! (Oliver Twist by Charles Dickens)*

snorted VERB slept ❑ *Or snorted we in the Seven Sleepers' den? (The Good-Morrow by John Donne)*

snuff NOUN snuff is tobacco in powder form which is taken by sniffing ❑

as he thrust his thumb and forefinger into the proffered snuff-box of the undertaker: which was an ingenious little model of a patent coffin. (*Oliver Twist* by Charles Dickens)

soliloquized VERB to soliloquize is when an actor in a play speaks to himself or herself rather than to another actor ❏ *"A new servitude! There is something in that," I soliloquized (mentally, be it understood; I did not talk aloud)* (*Jane Eyre* by Charlotte Brontë)

sough NOUN a sough is a drain or a ditch ❏ *as you may have noticed the sough that runs from the marshes* (*Wuthering Heights* by Emily Brontë)

spirits NOUN a spirit is the nonphysical part of a person which is believed to remain alive after their death ❏ *that I might raise up spirits when I please* (*Doctor Faustus 1.5* by Christopher Marlowe)

spleen ■ NOUN here spleen means a type of sadness or depression which was thought to only affect the wealthy ❏ *yet here I could plainly discover the true seeds of spleen* (*Gulliver's Travels* by Jonathan Swift) ■ NOUN irritability and low spirits ❏ *Adieu to disappointment and spleen* (*Pride and Prejudice* by Jane Austen)

spondulicks NOUN spondulicks is a slang word which means money ❏ *not for all his spondulicks and as much more on top of it* (*The Adventures of Huckleberry Finn* by Mark Twain)

stalled of VERB to be stalled of something is to be bored with it ❏ *I'm stalled of doing naught* (*Wuthering Heights* by Emily Brontë)

stanchion NOUN a stanchion is a pole or bar that stands upright and is used as a buidling support ❏ *and slid down a stanchion* (*The Adventures of Huckleberry Finn* by Mark Twain)

stang NOUN stang is another word for pole which was an old measurement ❏ *These fields were intermingled with woods of half a stang* (*Gulliver's Travels* by Jonathan Swift)

starlings NOUN a starling is a wall built around the pillars that support a bridge to protect the pillars ❏ *There were states of the tide when, having been down the river, I could not get back through the eddy-chafed arches and starlings of old London Bridge* (*Great Expectations* by Charles Dickens)

startings NOUN twitching or nighttime movements of the body ❏ *with midnight's startings* (*On His Mistress* by John Donne)

stomacher NOUN a panel at the front of a dress ❏ *but send her aunt the pattern of a stomacher* (*Emma* by Jane Austen)

stoop VERB swoop ❏ *Once a kite hovering over the garden made a swoop at me* (*Gulliver's Travels* by Jonathan Swift)

succedaneum NOUN a succedaneum is a substitute ❏ *But as a succedaneum* (*The Prelude* by William Wordsworth)

suet NOUN a hard animal fat used in cooking ❏ *and your jaws are too weak For anything tougher than suet* (*Alice's Adventures in Wonderland* by Lewis Carroll)

sultry ADJ sultry weather is hot and damp. Here sultry means unpleasant or risky ❏ *for it was getting pretty sultry for us* (*The Adventures of Huckleberry Finn* by Mark Twain)

summerset NOUN summerset is an old spelling of somersault. If someone does a somersault, they turn over completely in the air ❏ *I have seen him do the summerset* (*Gulliver's Travels* by Jonathan Swift)

supper NOUN supper was a light meal taken late in the evening. The main meal was dinner which was eaten at four or five in the afternoon ❏ *and the supper table was all set out* (*Emma* by Jane Austen)

surfeits VERB to surfeit in something is to have far too much of it, or to overindulge in it to an unhealthy degree ❏ *He surfeits upon cursed necromancy* (*Doctor Faustus chorus* by Christopher Marlowe)

surtout NOUN a surtout is a long close-fitting overcoat ❏ *He wore a long black surtout reaching nearly to his ankles* (*The Old Curiosity Shop* by Charles Dickens)

swath NOUN swath is the width of corn cut by a scythe ❏ *while thy hook Spares the next swath* (*Ode to Autumn* by John Keats)

sylvan ADJ sylvan means belonging to the woods ❏ *Sylvan historian* (*Ode on a Grecian Urn* by John Keats)

taction NOUN taction means touch. This means that the people had to be touched on the mouth or the ears to get their attention ❏ *without being roused by some external taction upon the organs of speech and hearing* (*Gulliver's Travels* by Jonathan Swift)

Tag and Rag and Bobtail PHRASE the riff-raff, or lower classes. Used in an insulting way ❏ *"No," said he; "not till it got about that there was no protection on the premises, and it come to be considered dangerous, with convicts and Tag and Rag and Bobtail going up and down."* (*Great Expectations* by Charles Dickens)

tallow NOUN tallow is hard animal fat that is used to make candles and soap ❏ *and a lot of tallow candles* (*The Adventures of Huckleberry Finn* by Mark Twain)

tan VERB to tan means to beat or whip ❏ *and if I catch you about that school I'll tan you good* (*The Adventures of Huckleberry Finn* by Mark Twain)

tanyard NOUN the tanyard is part of a tannery, which is a place where leather is made from animal skins ❏ *hid in the old tanyard* (*The Adventures of Huckleberry Finn* by Mark Twain)

tarry ADJ tarry means the colour of tar or black ❏ *his tarry pig-tail* (*Treasure Island* by Robert Louis Stevenson)

thereof PHRASE from there ❏ *By all desires which thereof did ensue* (*On His Mistress* by John Donne)

thick with, be PHRASE if you are 'thick with someone' you are very close, sharing secrets – it is often used to describe people who are planning something secret ❏ *Hasn't he been thick with Mr Heathcliff lately?* (*Wuthering Heights* by Emily Brontë)

thimble NOUN a thimble is a small cover used to protect the finger while sewing ❏ *The paper had been sealed in several places by a thimble* (*Treasure Island* by Robert Louis Stevenson)

thirtover ADJ thirtover is an old word which means obstinate or that someone is very determined to do want they want and can not be persuaded to do something in another way ❏ *I have been living on in a thirtover, lackadaisical way* (*Tess of the D'Urbervilles* by Thomas Hardy)

timbrel NOUN timbrel is a tambourine ❏ *What pipes and timbrels?* (*Ode on a Grecian Urn* by John Keats)

tin NOUN tin is slang for money/cash ❏ *Then the plain question is, an't it a pity that this state of things should continue, and how much better would it be for the old gentleman to hand over a reasonable amount of tin, and make it all right and comfortable* (*The Old Curiosity Shop* by Charles Dickens)

tincture NOUN a tincture is a medicine made with alcohol and a small amount of a drug ❏ *with ink composed of a cephalic tincture* (*Gulliver's Travels* by Jonathan Swift)

tithe NOUN a tithe is a tax paid to the church ❏ *and held farms which, speaking from a spiritual point of view, paid highly-desirable tithes* (*Silas Marner* by George Eliot)

towardly ADJ a towardly child is dutiful or obedient ❏ *and a towardly child* (*Gulliver's Travels* by Jonathan Swift)

toys NOUN trifles are things which are considered to have little importance, value, or significance ❏ *purchase my life from them bysome bracelets, glass rings, and other toys* (*Gulliver's Travels* by Jonathan Swift)

tract NOUN a tract is a religious pamphlet or leaflet ❏ *and Joe Harper got a hymn-book and a tract* (*The Adventures of Huckleberry Finn* by Mark Twain)

train-oil NOUN train-oil is oil from whale blubber ❏ *The train-oil and gunpowder were shoved out of sight in a minute* (*Wuthering Heights* by Emily Brontë)

tribulation NOUN tribulation means the suffering or difficulty you experience in a particular situation ❏ *Amy was learning this distinction through much tribulation* (*Little Women* by Louisa May Alcott)

trivet NOUN a trivet is a three-legged stand for resting a pot or kettle ❏ *a pocket-knife in his right; and a pewter pot on the trivet* (*Oliver Twist* by Charles Dickens)

trot line NOUN a trot line is a fishing line to which a row of smaller fishing lines are attached ❏ *when he got along I was hard at it taking up a trot line* (*The Adventures of Huckleberry Finn* by Mark Twain)

troth NOUN oath or pledge ❏ *I wonder, by my troth* (*The Good-Morrow* by John Donne)

truckle NOUN a truckle bedstead is a bed that is on wheels and can be slid under another bed to save space ❏ *It rose under my hand, and the door yielded. Looking in, I saw a lighted candle on a table, a bench, and a mattress on a truckle bedstead.* (*Great Expectations* by Charles Dickens)

trump NOUN a trump is a good, reliable person wo can be trusted ❏ *This lad Hawkins is a trump, I perceive* (*Treasure Island* by Robert Louis Stevenson)

tucker NOUN a tucker is a frilly lace collar which is worn around the neck ❏ *Whereat Scrooge's niece's sister the plump one with the lace tucker: not the one with the roses blushed.* (*A Christmas Carol* by Charles Dickens)

tureen NOUN a large bowl with a lid from which soup or vegetables are served ❏ *Waiting in a hot tureen!* (*Alice's Adventures in Wonderland* by Lewis Carroll)

turnkey NOUN a prison officer; jailer ❏ *As we came out of the prison through the lodge, I found that the great importance of my guardian was appreciated by the turnkeys, no less than by those whom they held in charge.* (*Great Expectations* by Charles Dickens)

turnpike NOUN the upkeep of many roads of the time was paid for by tolls (fees) collected at posts along the road. There was a gate to prevent people travelling further along the road until the toll had been paid. ❏ *Traddles, whom I have taken up by appointment at the turnpike, presents a dazzling combination of cream colour and light blue; and both he and Mr. Dick have a general effect about them of being all gloves.* (*David Copperfield* by Charles Dickens)

twas PHRASE it was ❏ *twas but a dream of thee* (*The Good-Morrow* by John Donne)

tyrannized VERB tyrannized means bullied or forced to do things against their will ❏ *for people would soon cease coming there to be tyrannized over and put down* (*Treasure Island* by Robert Louis Stevenson)

'un NOUN 'un is a slang term for one – usually used to refer to a person ❏ *She's been thinking the old 'un* (*David Copperfield* by Charles Dickens)

undistinguished ADJ undiscriminating or incapable of making a distinction between good and bad things ❑ *their undistinguished appetite to devour everything* (*Gulliver's Travels* by Jonathan Swift)

use NOUN habit ❑ *Though use make you apt to kill me* (*The Flea* by John Donne)

vacant ADJ vacant usually means empty, but here Wordsworth uses it to mean carefree ❑ *To vacant musing, unreproved neglect* (*The Prelude* by William Wordsworth)

valetudinarian NOUN one too concerned with his or her own health. ❑ *for having been a valetudinarian all his life* (*Emma* by Jane Austen)

vamp VERB vamp means to walk or tramp to somewhere ❑ *Well, vamp on to Marlott, will 'ee* (*Tess of the D'Urbervilles* by Thomas Hardy)

vapours NOUN the vapours is an old term which means unpleasant and strange thoughts, which make the person feel nervous and unhappy ❑ *and my head was full of vapours* (*Robinson Crusoe* by Daniel Defoe)

vegetables NOUN here vegetables means plants ❑ *the other vegetables are in the same proportion* (*Gulliver's Travels* by Jonathan Swift)

venturesome ADJ if you are venturesome you are willing to take risks ❑ *he must be either hopelessly stupid or a venturesome fool* (*Wuthering Heights* by Emily Brontë)

verily ADJ verily means really or truly ❑ *though I believe verily* (*Robinson Crusoe* by Daniel Defoe)

vicinage NOUN vicinage is an area or the residents of an area ❑ *and to his thought the whole vicinage was haunted by her.* (*Silas Marner* by George Eliot)

victuals NOUN victuals means food ❑ *grumble a little over the victuals* (*The Adventures of Huckleberry Finn* by Mark Twain)

vintage NOUN vintage in this context means wine ❑ *Oh, for a draught of*

vintage! (*Ode on a Nightingale* by John Keats)

virtual ADJ here virtual means powerful or strong ❑ *had virtual faith* (*The Prelude* by William Wordsworth)

vittles NOUN vittles is a slang word which means food ❑ *There never was such a woman for givin' away vittles and drink* (*Little Women* by Louisa May Alcott)

voided straight PHRASE voided straight is an old expression which means emptied immediately ❑ *see the rooms be voided straight* (*Doctor Faustus 4.1* by Christopher Marlowe)

wainscot NOUN wainscot is wood panel lining in a room so wainscoted means a room lined with wooden panels ❑ *in the dark wainscoted parlor* (*Silas Marner* by George Eliot)

walking the plank PHRASE walking the plank was a punishment in which a prisoner would be made to walk along a plank on the side of the ship and fall into the sea, where they would be abandoned ❑ *about hanging, and walking the plank* (*Treasure Island* by Robert Louis Stevenson)

want VERB want means to be lacking or short of ❑ *The next thing wanted was to get the picture framed* (*Emma* by Jane Austen)

wanting ADJ wanting means lacking or missing ❑ *wanting two fingers of the left hand* (*Treasure Island* by Robert Louis Stevenson)

wanting, I was not PHRASE I was not wanting means I did not fail ❑ *I was not wanting to lay a foundation of religious knowledge in his mind* (*Robinson Crusoe* by Daniel Defoe)

ward NOUN a ward is, usually, a child who has been put under the protection of the court or a guardian for his or her protection ❑ *I call the Wards in Jarndyce. The* *are caged up with all the others.* (*Bleak House* by Charles Dickens)

waylay VERB to waylay someone is to lie in wait for them or to intercept them ❑ *I must go up the road and waylay him* (*The Adventures of Huckleberry Finn* by Mark Twain)

weazen NOUN weazen is a slang word for throat. It actually means shrivelled ❑ *You with an uncle too! Why, I knowed you at Gargery's when you was so small a wolf that I could have took your weazen betwixt this finger and thumb and chucked you away dead* (*Great Expectations* by Charles Dickens)

wery ■ ADV very ❑ *Be wery careful o' vidders all your life* (*Pickwick Papers* by Charles Dickens) ■ *See* wibrated

wherry NOUN wherry is a small swift rowing boat for one person ❑ *It was flood tide when Daniel Quilp sat himself down in the wherry to cross to the opposite shore.* (*The Old Curiosity Shop* by Charles Dickens)

whether PREP whether means which of the two in this example ❑ *we came in full view of a great island or continent (for we knew not whether)* (*Gulliver's Travels* by Jonathan Swift)

whetstone NOUN a whetstone is a stone used to sharpen knives and other tools ❑ *I dropped pap's whetstone there too* (*The Adventures of Huckleberry Finn* by Mark Twain)

wibrated VERB in Dickens's use of the English language 'w' often replaces 'v' when he is reporting speech. So here 'wibrated' means 'vibrated'. In Pickwick Papers a judge asks Sam Weller (who constantly confuses the two letters) 'Do you spell it with a 'v' or a 'w'?' to which Weller replies 'That depends upon the taste and fancy of the speller, my Lord' ❑ *There are strings . . . in the human heart that had better not be wibrated'* (*Barnaby Rudge* by Charles Dickens)

wicket NOUN a wicket is a little door in a larger entrance ❑ *Having rested here, for a minute or so, to collect a good burst of sobs and an imposing show of tears and terror, he knocked loudly at the wicket;* (*Oliver Twist* by Charles Dickens)

without CONJ without means unless ❑ *You don't know about me, without you have read a book by the name of The Adventures of Tom Sawyer* (*The Adventures of Huckleberry Finn* by Mark Twain)

wittles ■ NOUN vittles is a slang word which means food ❑ *I live on broken wittles – and I sleep on the coals* (*David Copperfield* by Charles Dickens) ■ *See* wibrated

woo VERB courts or forms a proper relationship with ❑ *before it woo* (*The Flea* by John Donne)

words, to have PHRASE if you have words with someone you have a disagreement or an argument ❑ *I do not want to have words with a young thing like you.* (*Black Beauty* by Emily Brontë)

workhouse NOUN workhouses were places where the homeless were given food and a place to live in return for doing very hard work ❑ *And the Union workhouses? demanded Scrooge. Are they still in operation?* (*A Christmas Carol* by Charles Dickens)

yawl NOUN a yawl is a small boat kept on a bigger boat for short trips. Yawl is also the name for a small fishing boat ❑ *She sent out her yawl, and we went aboard* (*The Adventures of Huckleberry Finn* by Mark Twain)

yeomanry NOUN the yeomanry was a collective term for the middle classes involved in agriculture ❑ *The yeomanry are precisely the order of people with whom I feel I can have nothing to do* (*Emma* by Jane Austen)

yonder ADV yonder means over there ❑ *all in the same second we seem to hear low voices in yonder!* (*The Adventures of Huckleberry Finn* by Mark Twain)